# THE *Unforgettable* SPURGEON

C. H. Spurgeon's
attitudes, convictions, experiences and theology as
he recorded them in *The Sword and the Trowel*
(1865-1892)

**By**

ERIC HAYDEN

Other books about C. H. Spurgeon by Eric Hayden
**and available through Emerald House/Ambassador
Productions:**
*My Spurgeon Souvenirs*

## The Unforgettable Spurgeon

ISBN 1 889893 05 6

Published by
*Emerald House Group, Inc.*
1 Chick Springs Road, Suite 206
Greenville, South Carolina 29609
and
Ambassador Productions
16 Hillview Avenue
Belfast, Northern Ireland
BT5 6JH

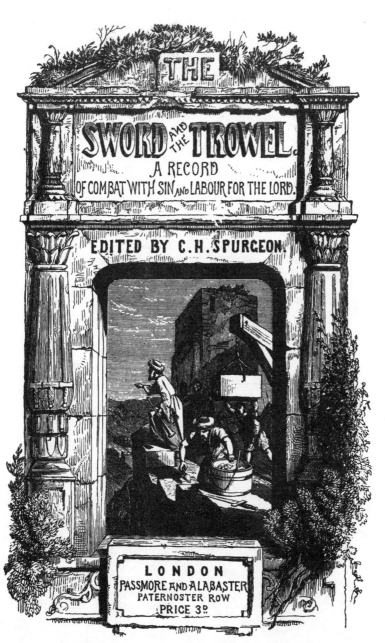

FACSIMILE OF FIRST COVER OF "THE SWORD AND THE TROWEL."

# CONTENTS

"The reader must forgive us if in our own magazine we become autobiographical."

C. H. Spurgeon
*The Sword and the Trowel*
1879, iii

"Many kind friends will have personal information about (the Editor), and think themselves injured if it is not given. Our relations with our readers are of a peculiarly fraternal kind, and therefore we are obliged to write matters which else might seem egotistical."

*The Sword and the Trowel*
886, 42

"*The Sword and the Trowel* has all along been a kind of biography of its Editor."

*The Sword and the Trowel*
1887, 146

# Introduction

Whenever the late Dr. Wilbur M. Smith called on me when I was pastor at the Metropolitan Tabernacle, London, he would always urge me to research the volumes of *The Sword and the Trowel* from 1865 to 1892, covering the lifetime of C. H. Spurgeon. He believed there could be no "definitive biography" of Spurgeon until this was done. Dr. Smith maintained that these magazines contained "a wealth of untapped material," especially in the monthly book reviews that would throw much light on the ministry, attitudes, convictions, experiences and theology of the great preacher and philanthropist.

I could not undertake such a task then as I had in mind a similar project from *The Metropolitan Tabernacle Pulpit* volumes. For me the sermons provided a searchlight beam, lighting up Spurgeon's life and ministry by revealing what he had said about himself. This resulted eventually in 1973 in the publication of *Searchlight on Spurgeon: "Spurgeon Speaks for Himself."*

It takes about ten years to read through these sermons, six volumes of the *New Park Street Pulpit* and fifty-six of the *Metropolitan Tabernacle Pulpit*. In busy pastorates how could I also find time to read twenty-seven volumes of *The Sword and the Trowel*? I decided to leave it for retirement, hoping nobody else did it first! It seems nobody has, for in the present-day biographies the authors have only referred to the magazines of Spurgeon when outlining and discussing the Down-Grade Controversy.

E. W. Bacon (*Spurgeon: Heir of the Puritans*) has only one mention of *The Sword and the Trowel*, in his chapter on the Down-Grade, and no mention of the magazines in *Books for Further Reading*.

Arnold Dallimore (*Spurgeon: a New Biography*) has but one footnoted mention of the magazine in his chapter on the Tabernacle, five mentions in "Training Young Preachers," two in "Spurgeonic Enterprises," one in "Mrs. Spurgeon," three in "Earnestly Contending for the Faith" and one in "Last Labours." That is a total of thirteen references in a book of 252 pages and no mention of the magazines in his "Annotated Bibliography."

Mike Nicholls (*C. H. Spurgeon: the Pastor Evangelist*) has eleven mentions of *The Sword and the Trowel* in the index but they are not listed in the bibliography.

Iain Murray (*The Forgotten Spurgeon*) has twenty-four references when dealing with the Down-Grade but only nine other mentions elsewhere in a book of 254 pages.

The most frequent uses of *The Sword and the Trowel* in a modern book about Spurgeon are by R. J. Sheehan in *C. H. Spurgeon and the Modern Church*, but his is not a biography of Spurgeon but a book giving "lessons for today from the Down-Grade Controversy."

No one can possibly give an authentic, let alone a balanced picture of Spurgeon without more detailed research into such a mine of personal information as the editor gave each month in his magazine. His views on annihilation, baptism, children, church officers, the Church of England, Calvinism, inquirers, fund-raising, hymnology, holidays, inspiration, music, Methodists, prophecy, Popery, prayer, the Plymouth Brethren, Quakers, revival, slavery, Sunday observance, theology, unity — all these and more can only be fully assessed with reference to his personal, autobiographical writing in *The Sword and the Trowel*.

Although I said I had left this research for retirement, I have, in fact, been doing it since boyhood! Sleeping in my father's den when we had visitors staying overnight, I often used to dip into the volumes of *The Sword and the Trowel* that lined the walls, some volumes being my father's and some my grandfather's. I think I was most intrigued by Spurgeon's lists of converts and baptisms and the resulting growth in membership of the Tabernacle. His reviews of children's books also caught my attention. Since then I have discovered much more gold in the mine and hope the reader will be thrilled and blessed as I share it with you.

*The Sword and the Trowel* was not, of course, Spurgeon's first venture into journalism. As a small child he planned his own magazine, writing most of the articles himself. While less than twelve years of age, he issued a 16-page, hand-written magazine only four inches by two and a quarter. Still at a day-school in Colchester, he edited some hundred of these magazines which he called *The Home Juvenile Society*, the first in April 1846. On page two, he appealed for contributors. He gave chapel news of prayer meetings and tea parties and also had a "humour corner" in which there were riddles and jokes. In some articles there were classical literary allusions.

In later years, he became joint-editor of *The Baptist Magazine* but he did not work too easily in double-harness. He resigned, stating that he was beginning a cheaper magazine. Thus, *The Sword and the Trowel* began in 1865 and was a great success from the first issue.

It began with the expansion of the Tabernacle's work into social areas like the Stockwell Orphanage and evangelistic outreach through the Colportage Association. Spurgeon felt that these and other Tabernacle Institutions should be brought before the general Christian public for their prayer support and financial backing. At the same time, he saw the need of the time was for spiritual reading and instruction for Christian families.

While the title of the magazine was taken from the familiar Old Testament story of Nehemiah rebuilding the walls of Jerusalem, he summarized it into *The Sword and the Trowel*. It was based on the words: "Every one with one of his hands in the work, and with the other held a weapon." His sub-title was more graphic: "A record of combat with sin and labour for the Lord." It was both battling and building, denouncing error in the religious world and bearing witness to God's truth.

From the publication of the first issue until just before his death Spurgeon edited the magazine, reading all the manuscripts sent by contributors, correcting proofs, reviewing a vast number of books (with some help from brother James) and writing a large proportion of the other material published month by month. Even when not healthy, recuperating at home or abroad, he carried on this editorial and journalistic work.

The magazine was once mentioned in the House of Lords, being referred to as "a lively newspaper." For twelve years after his death, much unpublished Spurgeon material was printed by subsequent editors.

To discover this mine of information is not merely to discover an unforgettable Victorian preacher; it fills in the gaps to be found in most biographies. The reader will discover, as I have already found out, that this will then correct the "we'll fit Spurgeon into our particular mould" attitude of some modern biographers. It will also hopefully put to rest once and for all some of the apocryphal stories about Spurgeon.

But most of all, while the volumes of *The Sword and the Trowel*, like The *Metropolitan Tabernacle Pulpit*, are being reprinted, Spurgeon will remain unforgettable. While some may refer to him as "forgotten," he will always be remembered as long as streets and roads are named after him (as in Norwood, South London), while his Tabernacle and College continue in existence and his former orphanage still ministers as Spurgeon's Child Care. Since the pen is mightier than the sword, the printed works of the Prince of Preachers will ensure that he is unforgettable throughout many countries in the world.

★

For the sake of not distracting the reader by printing reference numbers in the body of the text and at the bottom of pages as footnotes or referring him to a list of references relating to each chapter at the end of the book, I shall simply give the year and page number in brackets after the text itself, for example — (1867, 23).

## CHAPTER ONE

# Family and Friends

To the present day 2,800 inhabitants of Kelvedon, England Charles Haddon Spurgeon is the "unforgettable Spurgeon." On the wall of a cottage in the High Street of this Essex village is a memorial plaque to the great Victorian preacher stating that he was born there on June 19, 1834.

His ancestors had been sturdy Nonconformists for centuries, some of them Dutch refugees who escaped to England mid-way through the sixteenth century, because of the persecution of Protestants under the Duke of Alva.

Spurgeon's father, John, was an Independent (Congregational) pastor, his "tent-making" being that of a clerk in a coal yard. In his preaching, he was an evangelical Calvinist.

His mother, formerly Eliza Jarvis, had seventeen children in all, although nine of them died in infancy. Owing to hardship, baby Charles was sent to live with grandparents when he was only two-and-a-half years old. His parents had moved to Colchester, and he went to live with his grandfather who was also an Independent pastor, The Rev. James Spurgeon, minister at Stambourne. He, too, was a thorough-going Calvinist and gospel preacher.

At Stambourne, the young Spurgeon was looked after with much love and care. In the Manse, there was a wealth of Puritan literature which he was soon devouring before returning to his parents in Colchester at the age of seven. Even then summer holidays were spent with his grandparents. During those visits, he met a variety of visiting preachers who stayed at the Manse, notably Richard Knill whose prophecy is well known: "This child will one day preach the gospel, and he will preach it to great multitudes."

While at Stambourne he came under the care and attention of Aunt Ann, the unmarried daughter of James and Sarah

Spurgeon. It was Ann who first taught the boy Spurgeon to walk, talk, and read. She was only seventeen years of age, but her lively disposition was in sharp contrast to the rather somber atmosphere of the Manse. So by the age of five, he was reading aloud and praying at family prayers.

Back in Colchester, the atmosphere was different. His father was a most genial man with a ready wit, which was obviously passed on to Charles as was his strong preaching voice.

The young boy now had many younger friends and companions. He began day-school in a local dame-school and made many friends. Sadly many of them eventually went to the "big city" (London), and their lives became "a shipwreck." During his early days of schooling, he became aware of his sinfulness and lost all interest in games and pastimes. At fourteen, however, he was sent to the agricultural college in Maidstone with the idea of becoming a farmer. At fifteen, he left Maidstone to become a junior tutor at a school in Newmarket. There he became proficient in Latin and Greek, but importantly he became friends with the school cook. Mary King was elderly but that did not matter. In fact, in later years, when she retired to Ipswich, Spurgeon supplemented her income with a weekly allowance from his own pocket.

Mary was a strong Calvinist, and it was to her church in Newmarket that Spurgeon went. Back at school, they discussed the sermons together and it was from her that the young Spurgeon learned much about election, final perseverance and the necessity of godliness on the part of the converted. Spurgeon declared later that he learned more theology from her than from the minister! And this was before his own conversion experience.

Very rarely does Spurgeon write about his family and friends in the "Notes" he compiled each month in *The Sword and the Trowel*. He married his wife, Susannah and had twin sons, Tom and Charles, who are mentioned from time to time in connection with their Christian work and ministry. His parents and grandparents do, however, receive a mention from time to time, revealing the great affection he had for them. For instance, in the July "Notes" for 1883 he wrote:

It may not be thought unworthy of mention here that on Monday, May 14, our honoured father and mother were spared to celebrate their Golden Wedding Day with us at Westwood. All their children and grandchildren, and great-grandchildren were present, with the exception of our beloved son, Thomas, and the company consisted of thirty-two persons in all. Of this household seven are preachers of the gospel. Very gracious has the Lord been to us as a family, for from a remote ancestry the fear of God has ruled the house, and a blessing has rested upon it because of the ark of the Lord (1883, 332).*

After describing the way the past was reviewed with praise; the present was being enjoyed in a happy spirit of love and unity and looking forward to the future with hope and expectation, he went on:

Our own dear departed grandfather, so long an honoured winner of souls, used to rejoice in five of us as ministers of Christ, but now 'we are seven,' and there are others among us who occasionally bear witness for the truth in public. May all our friends have a like blessing, and may young people commencing life be wise enough to perceive that family piety and domestic happiness must go together: let them not expect the first without the second (Ibid).

One other friendship that was cemented in these early days was another unlikely one from the point of view of differing ages. This began soon after his conversion experience. He joined the church worshipping in St. Andrew's Street, Cambridge, a Baptist fellowship. At the first communion service he attended, he found nobody talked to him nor at the next time of fellowship around the table. On coming outside the church building, he spoke to an elderly man who had sat in the same pew; he emphasized that they were brothers in the Lord, professing that spiritual relationship by attending communion together. The man loosened and invited him to tea. The next Sunday he returned and continued to do so for some time.

* All references are to *The Sword and the Trowel*, first the **year**, then the **page** number.

Many years later Spurgeon and his old aquaintance were still firm friends in spite of the age difference.

About the same time, still only sixteen years of age, Spurgeon was asked to go with another friend on a preaching engagement in the country. Each thought the other was to be the preacher! When they discovered the quandary they were in, it was decided that Spurgeon should preach in the cottage meeting at Teversham. His "Sunday school address" was well received, and he continued his boy-preaching around the Fen district of Cambridgeshire. Soon he had his first convert, an experience he described as being like a diver coming up from the ocean depths with a precious pearl.

The Holy Spirit had been at work in his soul for some time then, culminating in his conversion experience. Godly grandfather and parents, the influence of the Puritans, the friendship of a humble Calvinistic cook, regular attendance at the House of God and diligent praying and Bible reading all culminated in his conversion which he wrote about in his own words in *The Sword and the Trowel.*

## CHAPTER TWO

# Conversion and Immersion

When lecturing on preaching, Spurgeon said something to the effect that an ounce of personal testimony was worth more than a ton of heavy theology, and when stuck for something to say, he put a charge of spiritual experience into the barrel and fired that. He certainly practiced what he preached. In every one of the fifty-six volumes of *The Metropolitan Tabernacle Pulpit* there is an account of his conversion, and the remarkable thing is that he repeated this account more frequently in the latter years of his ministry than at the beginning.

On Sunday morning January 6, 1850, a snowy day, he went out to his usual Congregational church in Colchester. Being unable to reach it, as the snow was falling more heavily, he turned down a side street where he saw a small Primitive Methodist Chapel. It was the place God had planned for him.

Only fifteen people were in the congregation, and the appointed preacher failed to arrive. Sitting beneath the gallery the teenage Spurgeon watched a thin man, perhaps a shoemaker, with little education or eloquence, enter the pulpit and read in a halting manner some verses from the book of Isaiah. He spoke a few words on the text, "Look unto Me, and be ye saved, all the ends of the earth, for I am God and there is none else" (Isaiah 45:22).

Not having much prepared to say, the layman repeated his text. After a few stumbling sentences, he looked at the stranger under the gallery and said, "Young man, you look very miserable, and you will always be miserable if you don't do as my text tells you, and that is, Look unto Christ." Shouting with might and main (as only a Methodist can said Spurgeon later), he called out, "Young man, look, in God's name look, and look now. Look! Look! Look! You have nothing to do but look and live."

Spurgeon said that he looked until he could have looked his

eyes away. He saw the way of salvation; he looked with repentance and faith to Jesus and entered into eternal life. He wanted to dance all the way home.

Although brought up a Congregationalist and converted in a Methodist chapel, through reading his Bible Spurgeon became convinced that true New Testament baptism was the immersion of a believer in water. After obtaining his parents' permission he, who had never even heard of Baptists until he was fourteen years of age, sought out a nearby Baptist pastor to baptize him. He gave the following account of his baptism in *The Sword and the Trowel*:

> Being called, in the providence of God, to live at Newmarket as usher in a school, I essayed to join myself to the church of believers in that town; but according to my reading of Holy Scripture, the believer in Christ should be buried with Him in baptism, and so enter upon his open Christian life. I cast about to find a Baptist minister, and I failed to find one nearer than Isleham, in the Fen country, where resided a certain Mr. W. W. Cantlow, who had once been a missionary in Jamaica but was then pastor of one of the Isleham Baptist churches. My parents wished me to follow my own convictions; Mr. Cantlow arranged to baptize me, and my employer gave me a day's holiday for the purpose.
>
> I can never forget the 3rd of May, 1850; it was my mother's birthday, and I myself was within a few weeks of being sixteen years of age. I was up early, to have a couple of hours for quiet prayer and dedication to God. Then I had some eight miles to walk to reach the spot where I was to be immersed into the Triune Name according to the sacred command. What a walk it was! What thoughts and prayers thronged my soul during that morning's journey! It was by no means a warm day and therefore all the better for the two or three hours of quiet foot-travel which I enjoyed. The sight of Mr. Cantlow's smiling face was a full reward for that country tramp. I think I see the good man now and the white ashes of the turf-fire by which we stood and talked together about the solemn exercise which lay before us.

We went together to the Ferry, for the Isleham friends had not degenerated to indoor immersion in a bath made by the art of man, but used the ampler baptistery of the flowing river.

Isleham Ferry, on the River Lark, is a very quiet spot, half-a-mile from the village and rarely disturbed by traffic at any time of the year. The river itself is a beautiful stream, dividing Cambridgeshire from Suffolk and is dear to local anglers. The navigation of this little River Lark is soon to be re-opened between Bury St. Edmunds and the sea at Lynn, but at Isleham it is more in its infancy.

The ferry-house, hidden in the picture by the trees, is freely opened for the convenience of minister and candidates at a baptizing. Where the barge is hauled up for repairs the preacher takes his stand when the baptizing is on a week-day and there are few spectators present. But on a Lord's Day, when great numbers are attracted, the preacher, standing in a barge moored mid-stream, speaks the Word to the crowds on both sides of the river. This can be done the more easily as the river is not very wide. Where three persons are seen at a stand is the usual place for entering the water. The right depth, with sure footing, may soon be found, and so the delightful service proceeds in the gently flowing stream. No accident or disorder has ever marred the proceedings. In the course of seven or eight miles the Lark serves no fewer than five Baptist churches, and they would on no account give up baptizing out-of-doors.

The first baptizing at Isleham is recorded thus: "Sept. 13, 1798. John Webber, Sn., John Webber, Jr., William Brown, John Wibrow and Mary Gunstone were baptized by Mr. Fuller, of Kettering, at Isleham Ferry."

To me there seemed to be a great concourse on that week-day. Dressed, I believe, in a jacket with a boy's turn-down collar, I attended the service previous to the ordinance; but all remembrance of it has gone from me: my thoughts were in the water, sometimes with my Lord in joy, and sometimes with myself in trembling awe at making so public a confession. There were first to be baptized two women, Diana Wilkinson and Eunice Fuller, and I was asked to conduct them through the water to the minister, but this I most timidly declined. It was a new experience to me, never having seen a baptism before, and I was afraid of making some mistake. The wind blew down the river with a cutting blast as my turn came to wade into the flood, but after I had walked a few steps and noted the people on the ferry-boat and in boats and on either shore, I felt as if heaven and earth and hell might all gaze upon me, for I was not ashamed, there and then, to own myself a follower of the Lamb. Timidity was gone; I have scarcely met with it since. I lost a thousand fears in that River Lark and found that "in keeping His commandments there is great reward." It was a thrice-happy day to me. God be praised for the preserving goodness which allows me to write of it with delight at the distance of forty years!

> MANY DAYS HAVE PASSED SINCE THEN,
> MANY CHANGES I HAVE SEEN;
> YET HAVE BEEN UPHELD TILL NOW;
> WHO COULD HOLD ME UP BUT THOU?

I am indebted to Mr. Wilson, the present pastor of Isleham, for the following note, which reminds me of an excellent companion I had almost forgotten:

Mr. W. H. Cantlow, a worthy Baptist deacon at Ipswich, well remembers, when a boy at school, walking with Mr. Spurgeon from Newmarket to Isleham--a distance of eight miles to be at the baptism. He says, "I often think of the earnest talks he had with me and always remember one remark he made on our way to the week-night service about the need of obtaining spiritual food during the week, as it was so long to have to wait from one Sunday to the other.

The recollection of the service at the river-side is fondly cherished by several still living who rejoice that they were there. But the most precious memory of that day is the prayer-meeting in the vestry in the evening where Mr. Spurgeon prayed, and people wondered and wept for joy as they listened to the lad. One may be excused for envying those who were there.

In front of the new school-room, adjoining the chapel, is the following inscription:

---

*This Stone was Laid on September 19th, 1888,*

*By Mr. G. Apthorpe, in Memory of the late*

*Rev. W. W. Cantlow,*

*Who, while Pastor of the Church, Baptized the*

*Rev. C. H. Spurgeon,*

*At Isleham Ferry, on May 3rd, 1850.*

---

Mr. Cantlow's grave is only a few yards off.

Mr. Wilson also explains our engraving and adds an amusing story:

In the view of the Ferry, the chaise and cart are waiting to cross the river by the ferry-boat. One old lighter is rotting away in the water, and another lies high and dry under repair. The box is for keeping eels until they can be sent to market, and the long pole is for crossing the river in the small boat, which is also to be seen if you look for it. We shall sell photographs of the Ferry for our Building Fund. They can be had of me at Isleham, or at the Tabernacle, price 2s. 6d. each.

To conclude: The late vicar, a very solemn man, meeting a deacon of ready wit at the Ferry, began to find fault with a recent baptizing there. Said the vicar, "I suppose this is the place were the people came crowding the other Sunday, showing the little respect they had for the Sabbath day."

"There was, indeed, a great crowd," replied the deacon, "but they were all as still and attentive as in the house of God." "Is it true that the man J. S. was baptized?" enquired the vicar. "Yes, quite true," said the deacon, "and he seemed to be full of joy at the time." "What!" exclaimed the vicar, "a man who never went to school, and cannot read a word! How much can he know about the religion he came here to profess?" "Well," answered the deacon, with a smile, "Very likely the poor man knows little as yet."

"Still, he told us how he found the Saviour and became happy in His love. But," added the deacon, "Do not you, sir, christen little children, declaring that you make them children of God while you are perfectly aware that the children know nothing at all?

If any ask—Why was I thus baptized? I answer because I believed it to be an ordinance of Christ, very specially joined by Him with faith in His name. "He that believeth and is baptized shall be saved." I had no superstitious idea that baptism would save me, for I was saved. I did not seek to have sin washed away by water, for I believed that my sins were forgiven me through faith in Christ Jesus.

Yet I regarded baptism as the token to the believer of cleansing, the emblem of his burial with his Lord and the outward avowal of his new birth. I did not trust in it, but because I trusted in Jesus as my Saviour, I felt bound to obey Him as my Lord and follow the example which He set us in Jordan in His own baptism. I did not fulfill the outward ordinance to join a party and become a Baptist but to be a Christian after the apostolic fashion; for they, when they believed, were baptized.

It is now questioned whether John Bunyan was baptized, but the same question can never be raised concerning me. I, who scarcely belong to any sect, am nevertheless, by no means willing to have it doubted in time to come whether or not I followed the conviction of my heart. I read the New Testament for myself and saw Believers' Baptism there, and I had no mind to neglect what I saw to be the Lord's order. If others see not as I do, to their own Master they stand or fall, but for me the perceptions of my understanding in spiritual things were the law of my life, and I hope they will always be so. Dear reader, let us follow the Lamb withersoever He goeth!" (1890, 157).

Although there is no written account of Spurgeon's conversion in *The Sword and the Trowel*, there are several comments about conversion.

Closing the Monday evening prayer meeting at the Tabernacle on August 4, 1890 he referred to the expression which several people had used when speaking to him of their conversion — "I gave my heart to Jesus." He commented that he "was not going to censure them for using that expression, but he wished to remind them that it is not what we give to Jesus that saves us, but what Jesus

ISLEHAM FERRY ON THE RIVER LARK, WHERE C. H. SPURGEON
WAS BAPTIZED, MAY 3, 1850.

gives to us. We have to receive Jesus, to accept Him as God has set Him forth, as our Surety and Substitute. When we have received Christ by faith, love follows as a natural result. Trusting in Jesus, we must love Him; and "we love Him because He first loved us"

> Tis not that I did choose thee,
> For, Lord, that could not be;
> This heart would still refuse thee,
> But thou has chosen me.

(1890, 539)

In Artillery Street, Colchester, Spurgeon received Christ by faith, he did not choose Him.

Reviewing a book by the Religious Tract Society, *The Problem of Life*, in the Review Notices of the magazine, Spurgeon stressed:

> Very few men ever reach faith through being argued with; half an hour's prayer to God has frequently done more than night after night of discussion. In numbers of instances the head will be right as soon as the heart is renewed, and the way to win the assent of the understanding is to secure the consent of the affections.(1876, 480)

Certainly it was Spurgeon's heart and not his head that was appealed to in that Colchester Primitive Methodist Chapel. The almost illiterate lay preacher was well-nigh incapable of preaching a logical discourse seeking to win over his hearers' heads.

At his baptism the cutting wind blew across the ferry crossing on the River Lark. Did that come to mind when he was reviewing a book in his magazine entitled *The Story of the First Four Centuries*? After some comments on the excellency of the production and its readable style he said,

> The author, we observe, admits baptism was by immersion, but thinks this was on account of "the warm climate of the East." Our readers will, perhaps, do the early Christians more justice, and ascribe it to their desire to obey strictly the Master's will. (1865, 77)

Since Spurgeon was a teenager when baptized by immersion and the other candidates were mature women, he had little time for those who baptized infants. Reviewing *The Theology of the New Testament* he commented:

> We of course demur to the author's exposition of baptism. He says, "Infant baptism is in Paul's epistles just as little forbidden as enjoined." Quite true, for he had no commission to enjoin it, and no one had then thought of it, so that there was no need to suggest the error by condemning it. The author in the same sentence says that he (Paul), however, lays evident stress upon the fact that "there is but one baptism, as there is but one saving faith." So say we, and we therefore keep to the immersion of believers and reject so different an ordinance as the "Rantising of Infants". (1871, 43)

In a children's book, *A.L.O.E.*'s *Sunday Picture Book* he criticizes the artist for representing John the Baptist as pouring water on Christ's head. "We never read of his doing that. The Orientals pour oil on the head, but we do not think that they ever anoint with water." (1872, 46)

He was always willing, not only to listen, but to publish the other side. This he did in *The Sword and the Trowel* by reprinting "The Baptismal Service Practically Considered" (extracted from *The Irish Church Advocate*). It was a reply to Spurgeon's own sermon on Baptismal Regeneration. His editor's comment was: "If our antagonists will only keep on answering us in this way we shall not need to utter another syllable!" (1875, 413)

Not all Church of England clergymen were against Spurgeon in this baptism controversy. Bishop Charles J. Ellicott in *A New Testament Commentary for English Readers*, which Spurgeon reviewed, stated that in the incident of Philip and the Eunuch "They went down both into the water. The Greek preposition might mean simply unto the water, but the universality of immersion in the practice of the early church supports the English version. The eunuch would lay aside his garments, descend chest-deep into the water, and be plunged under it." (1880, 132)

In an "In Memoriam" column Spurgeon spoke highly of one Church of England clergyman as "Our dear brother, Rev. Robert Curme, vicar of Sandford, Oxon . . . a sweet Christian, of calm and serene spirit, full of love, and humility, yet firm as a rock in the doctrine of grace. When the denouncer of Baptismal Regeneration was shunned by many of the clergy, one of his brethren asked Mr. Curme, "How can you spend so much time in the company of Spurgeon?" His answer was, "It is more wonderful that he should associate with me than that I should meet with him." (1884, 442)

He was not so charitable about Hugh Price Hughes.

> Mr. Spurgeon never taught, or even believed, in any dogma of adult baptism; but in the baptism of believers, whether juvenile or adult. This is a very important difference, and we beg Mr. Hughes in future to observe it." (1886, 194)

Naturally Spurgeon's views about believers' baptism by immersion were most strongly expressed and expounded when he preached upon the subject. Nevertheless these written comments in *The Sword and the Trowel* add further insight to Spurgeon's views and defence of a doctrine he held dear. Perhaps he summed up his views most concisely in these words when reviewing a book entitled *The Minister of Baptism* (A history of church opinion from the time of the apostles). Spurgeon wrote:

> Here are the facts as we see them: the whole Church of Christ is a priesthood; we have not a word in Holy Scripture concerning any hierarchy within her pale. Sprinkling is not baptism in any case. Only believers should be baptized. The baptism of an unbeliever is no baptism into Christ. The true church derives her life from the indwelling Spirit and not from any imaginary transmission of occult power from man to man. To pretend that none can be saved unless baptized by certain ordained individuals is to degrade the truth of God into a priestcraft almost heathenish in its superstition. All this mess and muddle which arises out of the inventions with which God's simple Word is overlaid is only worthy to be sport for the children in the streets of the New Jerusalem. We hold in high esteem our brethren who differ from us and yet live by faith in Christ Jesus . . . it is ours to preach the gospel and immerse believers; and in this they do not compete with us. Our spheres do not clash; we can afford to dwell apart. (1890, 144)

## CHAPTER THREE

# Preaching and Pastoring

Young Spurgeon's early attempts at preaching in the villages around Cambridge were under the auspices of the St. Andrews Street Baptist Church's lay preacher's association. James Vinter organized the rota of engagements and was nicknamed "The Bishop." Vinter had recognized the young Spurgeon's speaking ability through hearing him give Sunday school addresses. The association arranged for lay preachers to visit thirteen village chapels, and Charles was soon being asked for a return visit. He was busy with day-school work each day of the week so it is difficult to grasp how he found time for sermon preparation for the many preaching engagements now coming his way--weeknights as well as Sundays.

In a short address given in later years to the Metropolitan Tabernacle Country Mission entitled "Young Preachers Encouraged" he let us into the secret:

It is an admirable thing for young men to begin early to preach the truth, for it is the best way of learning it. My college course was after this fashion. I was for three years a Cambridge man, though I never entered the university. I could not have obtained a degree because I was a Nonconformist; and, moreover, it was a better thing for me to pursue my studies under an admirable scholar and tender friend and preach at the same time. I was, by my tutor's often expressed verdict, considered to be sufficiently proficient in my studies to have taken a good place on the list had the way been open. "You could win at a canter," said he to me. I had, however, a better college course, for I studied theology as much as possible during the day, and then at five in the evening I became a travelling preacher and started into the villages to tell out what I had learned. My quiet meditation during the walk helped me to digest what I had read, and the rehearsal of my lesson in public, by preaching it to the people, fixed it on my memory. I do not mean that I ever repeated a single sentence from memory, but I thought my reading over again while on my legs and thus worked it into my very soul. I must have been a singular-looking youth on wet evenings.

During the last year of my stay in Cambridge, when I had given up my office as usher, I was wont to sally forth every night in the week except on Saturday and walk three, five or perhaps eight miles out and back again on my preaching work, and when it rained I encased myself in waterproof leggings and a mackintosh coat and a hat with a waterproof covering, and I carried a dark lantern to show me the way across the fields. I had many adventures of which I will not now speak, but the point is that what I had gathered by my studies during the day I handed out to a company of villagers in the evening and was greatly profited by the exercise. I always found it good to say my lesson when I had learned it; children do that, you know, and it is equally good for preachers, especially if they say their lesson by heart. (1881, 5)

In the very first volume of *The Sword and the Trowel*, reviewing a book by R. W. Dale (*The Jewish Temple and the Christian Church*) Spurgeon states his preference for one particular kind of preaching:

The expository style is much to be commended; occasionally at least, and especially at different intervals on one part of the Sabbath-day. (1865, 177)

Much of his early preaching was in the open air--a practice he later commended to the students of his pastors' college. Writing his magazine "Notes" for the month of July, he advised:

Now is the time for open-air preaching. No minister should keep within the walls of a building when he can preach the gospel upon the beautiful green sward with the blue heavens above him. Brethren, come out of your dens and corners and make the gospel to be heard by those who are ignorant of it. Fishermen do not wait for the fish to swim to them, but they go after them. Turn out into the highways and hedges and compel the people to come in. (1874, 341)

Instancing His Lord as our example, for He trained and chose seventy others to do the same work, he wrote:

"As ye go, preach the gospel." Did He shave the head of one of them to make him a priest? Did He decorate one of them to say mass--to swing a censer or to elevate the host? Did He instruct one of them to regenerate children by baptism? Did He bring one of them up to chant in surplices and march in processions? No, those things He never thought of and neither will we. If He had thought of them, it would only have been with utter contempt, for what is there in such childish things? The preaching of the cross--this it is which is to them that perish foolishness but unto us who are saved it is the wisdom of God and the power of God; for it pleaseth God by the foolishness of preaching to save them that believe. (1877, 494)

It was this kind of preaching that resulted in his being called to Waterbeach Chapel. After preaching one Sunday in October 1851, he was given an urgent invitation to return. After this return visit he was invited to become pastor. He accepted although he was only seventeen years of age. He resigned his school-teaching but continued to live in Cambridge. Soon he was preaching to a crowded chapel every Sunday. People came from the surrounding villages as well as from Waterbeach itself. The original forty membership became four hundred! Doors and windows were left open so that people could hear the services outside. He did not think that evangelistic preaching was the key to success for every preacher in every place:

We do not hold that the preaching of the gospel will always fill a place of worship. That belief would involve an unjust condemnation of many faithful men. But we do say that, other things being equal, no theme is so permanently attractive as the grand old gospel, and if a man cannot fill a place by preaching it, why then it does not go to be filled; or if it can be filled by other talk, no good will come of such a filling. (1888, 43)

His suggestion for success was rather that men should preach their old sermons:

I do not mean the same sermons but with the same force as when we began to "Tell to sinners round, What a dear Saviour we have found." I would like to preach again as I did at first, only a great deal better. I intensely believed and meant every word I spoke; I do so now, but doubts will arise now which never vexed me then. I would like to be a child again before the Lord, and to keep so, for I am sure that questions and doubts are a sad loss to any man. (1880, 322)

He knew the value of encouragement. Addressing the Tabernacle's Country Mission he said:

I am not old enough to have forgotten the struggles of my own early days or the influence of a cheering word upon my young heart, and so I take a loving and lively interest in those who sincerely endeavour to do their best for their Master, even though that best be raw and uncouth. (1881, 4)

During his time at Waterbeach he recognized his gift for pastoral concern, and this spark of recognition was soon fanned into a flame. He talked to men and women in the street, showing his interest in them and his understanding of their problems. He visited them in their homes and soon knew the names of the children of the household. He prayed with them when ill and comforted them when sorrowing. Both publically and privately he preached the gospel.

This pastoral visitation was again a feature of his London ministry even when his life was in danger through a raging cholera epidemic. But first we must see how the call came to the London pastorate in New Park Street Chapel, Southwark. In *The Sword and the Trowel* we can read about it as it was described by Spurgeon after a gap of twenty-five years:

We walked on a Sabbath morning, according to our wont, from Cambridge to the village of Waterbeach in order to occupy the pulpit of the little Baptist Chapel. It was a country road, and there were four or five honest miles of it which we usually measured each Sunday foot by foot, unless we happened to be met by a certain little pony and cart which came half way but could not by any possibility venture further because of the enormous expense which would have been incurred by driving through the toll-gate at Milton. That winter's morning we were all aglow with our walk and ready for our pulpit exercises.

Sitting down in the table-pew, a letter was passed to us bearing the postmark of London. It was an unusual missive and was opened with curiosity. It contained an invitation to preach at New Park Street Chapel, Southwark, the pulpit of which had formerly been occupied by Dr. Rippon--the very Dr. Rippon whose hymn-book was then before us upon the table, the great Dr. Rippon out of whose Selection we were about to choose hymns for our worship. The late Dr. Rippon seemed to hover over us as an immeasurably great man-- the glory of whose name covered New Park Street Chapel and its pulpit with awe unspeakable.

We quietly passed the letter across the table to the deacon who gave out the hymns observing that there was some mistake and that the letter must have been intended for a Mr. Spurgeon who preached somewhere down in Norfolk. He shook his head and observed that he was afraid there was no mistake as he always knew that his minister would be run away with by some large church or other but that he was a little surprised that the Londoners should have heard of him quite so soon. "Had it been Cottenham or St. Ives or Huntingdon," said he, "I should not have wondered at all, but going to London is rather a great step from this little place." He shook his head very gravely; but the time was come for us to look out the hymns, and therefore the letter was put away and, as far as we can remember, was for the day quite forgotten even as a dead man out of mind.

On the following Monday an answer was sent to London, informing the deacon of the church at Park Street that he had fallen into an error in directing his letter to Waterbeach, for the Baptist minister of that village was very little more than nineteen years of age and quite unqualified to occupy a London pulpit. In due time came another epistle setting forth that the former letter had been written in perfect knowledge of the young preacher's age and had been intended for him and him alone. The request of the former letter was repeated and pressed, a date mentioned for the journey to London and the place appointed at which the preacher would find lodging. That invitation was accepted, and as the result thereof the boy preacher of the Fens took his post in London. (1879, 1 & 2)

Just as he had had his doubts in the vestry at Waterbeach, so he had as he made his way to preach at New Park Street Chapel with a view that he felt unequal to the task:

At sight of Park Street Chapel we felt for a moment amazed at our own temerity, for it seemed to our eyes to be a large, ornate and imposing structure, suggesting an audience wealthy and critical and far removed from the humble folk to whom our ministry had been sweetness and light. It was early, so there were no persons entering, and when the set time was fully come there were no signs to support the suggestion raised by the exterior of the building, and we felt that by God's help we were not yet out of our depth, and were not likely to be with so small an audience. The Lord helped us very graciously; we had a happy Sabbath in the pulpit and spent the intervals with warm-hearted friends, and when at night we trudged back to the Queen Square narrow lodging we were not alone, and we no longer looked on Londoners as flinty-hearted barbarians. Our tone was altered; we wanted no pity of anyone; we did not care a penny for the young gentlemen lodgers and their miraculous ministers nor for the grind of the cabs nor for anything else under the sun. The lion had been looked at all round, and his majesty did not appear to be a tenth as majestic as when we had only heard his roar miles away. (Ibid., 3)

Once the "lion" was conquered and the call accepted, Spurgeon's London pastorate began. It was February 1854, and he was still a teenager--nineteen years of age. Within a month the building was crowded with every seat occupied and many standing in available spaces with others sitting in window sills.

When the deacons brought up the question of ordination, he would not agree, for he had received "the ordination of the pierced hand." It was never mentioned again. He personally rejected the title "Reverend," although he later used it "for the sake of the postman!" By then his publishers were using it on the printed sermons, and even when he asked them to refrain from doing so, it was still printed on the annual reports of some of his institutions. He much preferred the title "Pastor." Even in 1891, the year before his death, "Rev." appeared on the Annual Report of the Colportage Association.

And so, unordained, non-collegiate trained but Spirit-filled, the boy-preacher from the Fens began his London ministry, and New Park Street Chapel went on from strength to strength. Within months the building was being enlarged. While the refurbishment was in progress the congregation met in the Exeter Hall on the Strand. Although this hall seated 4,000 with room for another 1,000 to stand, hundreds were turned away. Thus the enlarged chapel, now seating 1,500, was far too small.

After a time he was denied further use of the Exeter Hall and transferred to the Surrey Gardens Music Hall. This had a crowd capacity of 10,000, but Spurgeon filled it. One evening some trouble-makers falsely shouted "Fire!" and the resulting panic caused seven deaths; and twenty-eight others were injured and needed hospital treatment. Spurgeon had to go into retreat to prevent a breakdown, and they managed to keep from him the newspaper reports--many of them cruel in their criticism. After eight days he was able to resume his ministry at New Park Street Chapel. He organized a fund to help victims of the disaster and visited the hospitals and homes of the bereaved and suffering.

For three years Spurgeon continued to preach in the Music Hall on Sunday mornings; he held the evening service in the chapel. One biographer entitles his chapter describing this period as "Revival Comes to London."

After two years in London Spurgeon and his deacons saw that there was only one thing to be done--a large new church building must be built. Before, however, we look at this thrilling enterprise we know as the Metropolitan Tabernacle, there is

THE ROYAL SURREY GARDENS MUSIC HALL—
THE SCENE OF THE GREAT DISASTER ON OCTOBER 19, 1856.

one touching reference to those early London days which he made in his "Notes" many years later. Amidst all the rich and famous he often wrote about in these "Notes" he had room for "a sister unknown to fame, beyond the Tabernacle" who had just died.

> Mrs. Hooper at the age of eighty-seven finished an earnest, faithful life of service and of suffering. We lodged with her when first we came to London, and we cannot forget her kindness in those early days. She was true to the core, and to the best of her ability served her Lord and the church. (1887, 437)

MR. SPURGEON AT THE AGE OF TWENTY-THREE

## CHAPTER FOUR

# Stones and "Living Stones"

After building work had been going on for two years, Spurgeon's Metropolitan Tabernacle was opened in Newington Butts, Elephant and Castle, London. The opening day was March 25, 1861. It was "Metropolitan" because it was situated in the Metropolis; it was a "Tabernacle" because God's people are always on the march. The first service was held on Sunday, March 31, 1861.

The Metropolitan Tabernacle

### The Building

The total cost of the building project was £31,322 (Spurgeon himself contributed over £5,000), and it was opened free from debt. That amount of money works out at approximately £1,000 for every year of Spurgeon's ministry.

It was built on Grecian lines and not Gothic, since Greek is the language of the New Testament. At that time it was considered the largest non-conformist building in the world.

Some present-day authors have suggested that Spurgeon designed the Tabernacle himself. This was not so. He chose the

Grecian style and chose the name, but a competition was held for architects to send in their plans. £50 was the prize offered for the winning entry. Over 250 architects applied for details of the competition. The final date for entries resulted in sixty-two plans and one model. The winner was chosen by the designers voting among themselves. But the building committee chose the winner of the second prize with Spurgeon requesting that four towers, one at each corner of the building, be dispensed with since nobody could sit in them.

Several biographers differ about the seating capacity of the Tabernacle. Some forget the seat-flaps on the end of the pews, allowing another 1000 to be seated. So let Spurgeon's *The Sword and the Trowel* clarify the matter once and for all.

> (It) seats 5,500 and holds 6,500 (and) has been filled from the day it was opened unto the present time. (1865, 30)

The same "Note" states that the building was constructed as large as possible "within the natural compass of the voice of the preacher."

## The Membership

When Pastor and members moved into the new Tabernacle, the membership was 1,250. But they took a whole new congregation with them collected from the Sunday services held in the Exeter Hall, Surrey Gardens Music Hall and the Crystal Palace. A month after the new building was opened seventy-seven applied for baptism and membership, seventy-two the month after that and 121 the month following. Growth continued through the thirty-odd years of Spurgeon's ministry until in the year of his death the membership numbered more than the seating capacity. Spurgeon commented in his "Notes,"

> . . . Where could we put more people if we had them? The building will not provide accommodation for more, though it is quite large enough for one man to fill. Taking off the free seats, we have not sittings for all the present members if they were to come at one time. (1890, 198)

Within four years of the opening of the Tabernacle the membership was 2,881 of which forty-seven had become ministers of the gospel, seven had become city missionaries, and three were Bible women. When Spurgeon interviewed applicants for membership he always asked them, "If you become a member of this church, what form of Christian service will you undertake?" He did not believe in carrying passengers on his ship--all were to be crew members!

Applicants were well vetted.

Candidates for church membership have an interview with one of the Elders, some of whom attend the Tabernacle for that purpose every Wednesday evening. A record is made by that Elder of the result of that interview in what is called the Inquirers' Book. If satisfied with the candidate, he gives a card which qualifies for direct meeting with Mr. Spurgeon who devotes a fixed proportion of his time to that office. If Mr. Spurgeon thinks favourably of the individual, the name is announced at a church meeting, and visitors are appointed to make the most careful inquiries into the whole circumstances connected with the application. If this investigation is satisfactory, the candidate appears at a church meeting where he is examined by the Pastor after which he retires, and the visitor gives his report upon the case. It is then proposed to the church for its adoption, and if approved, the Pastor gives the right hand of fellowship. As soon after this as convenient, the candidate is baptized, and on the next first Sabbath in the month ensuing unites in the Communion Service, having first been recognized before the whole church by again receiving from the Pastor the right hand of fellowship. (1865, 31)

Spurgeon was well aware of the days when church members merely occupied a seat in church and left the running of the church and its witness to the world outside to a faithful few. He wrote in his magazine under the title: "The Church, a Hive of Busy Workers:"

We are still suffering from the inertia of past days when the whole duty of man was considered to have been fulfilled if the church rules were subscribed to and a seat was taken and constant attendance was kept up. We have done with such idle ideas. Our ministers must teach members that the church ought to be a hive of busy workers, that Christ should be honoured in the family and in the workshop and that when a Christian ceases to be aggressively useful, his spiritual life becomes a matter of question. (1870, 222)

## The Leadership

The charismatic of today who thinks he has discovered or rediscovered the New Testament pattern of shared leadership in the church must think again. "There is nothing new under the sun," said wise king Solomon. Spurgeon knew of and practiced shared leadership. The officers of the Tabernacle consisted of Pastor, Assistant Teacher, Deacons and Elders. There were ten deacons (why not the scriptural number of seven we wonder), and these were all chosen for lifelong service. Their duty was to look after the temporal interests of the church (fabric and finance). There were twenty-three elders who were elected annually. Their duty was the spiritual interests of the church (pastoral and teaching). This form of government is, we believe, in harmony with that which in similar circumstances existed in the primitive churches. (*The Sword and the Trowel* by G. R., 1865, 31)

One of the most frequent apocryphal sayings attributed to Spurgeon is about deacons. He strongly denied it in his magazine:

We ourselves are charged with having said that "a deacon is worse than a devil, for if you resist the devil he will flee from you, but if you resist a deacon he will fly at you." This is no saying of ours; we never had any cause to speak so severely, and although in some cases it is undoubtedly true, we have never had any experimental proof of it. Not one in a hundred of all the sayings upon us are ours at all,

and as to this one it was in vogue before we were born.
(1868, 243)

His true opinion was: "Our observation of deacons leads us
to observe that, as a rule, they are quite as good men as the pastors,
and the bad and good in the ministry and the diaconate are to be
found in very much the same proportions. (Ibid)

Some years later he amplified what he had said when
commenting on an American article entitled "The Hornless
Deacon."

There is no accounting for our Transatlantic cousins . . .
deacons do not possess horns and hoofs. Some pastors,
when hardly driven, have thought they did, but this was
a clerical error. We believe that all evil reports about
deacons arise from nightmare and are slanderous and
absurd, but still they do arise . . . Our own opinion is that
when deacons have horns it will generally be found that
the minister has a tail. There is six of one and half-a-dozen
of the other in most cases of disagreement between the
two classes of church-officers. (1880, 9)

On the credit side he was able to add:

Certainly we know of deacons who from year to year plod
away at the Pastor's side, glad to perform services of any
kind so long as God is glorified, and the church is
prospered. Seldom are their names mentioned in public,
and yet they are the mainstay of the church, the regulators
of her order and the guardians of her interests. (Ibid, 10)

Of deacons' meetings and church business meetings (the bug-
bear of many a present-day pastor) he had this to say, when
reviewing "Some of the Great Preachers of Wales:"

We have felt inclined to envy this holy man (Daniel
Rowlands) upon one special point: he would have
nothing to do with the management of the church or the
chapel in which it met. He kept himself to his preaching,
came in through a door in the back wall of the meeting-
house and disappeared suddenly when he had done

without being worried with petty quarrels and idle tales. Of course we dare not imitate him in this, for in doing so we should neglect grave duties, but oh, that we could! A man in such a case ought to preach like an angel. Alas! the service of tables and of a great many other things overload some of us and make us groan for deliverance. (1886, 83)

Perhaps this is why he made his brother, James Archer Spurgeon, his co-pastor and allowed him to take many of the administrative jobs onto his shoulders.

## The Ordinances

The majority of present-day Baptist churches have a baptistry in the floor that is covered over, except when in use, with heavy boards. On top are usually the communion table and deacons' chairs. In a few cases we have a modern building where the baptistry is open all the time. Often this covered over method is a space-saver. One London Church surmounts the difficulty by covering the baptistry with thick armour-plated glass. On top is a communion table, the top of which is also glass so that it is possible to see right through it into the baptizing pool.

This would not have done for Spurgeon. He believed that architectural design should be governed by New Testament theology, and so he had an open baptistry in the Metropolitan Tabernacle.

When the third Tabernacle was built after being bombed during the Second World War, American plans for an elevated baptistry were flown over. Again it had a glass front and could be seen at all times. But it is now once again situated in the floor, unseen except when in use. Spurgeon would have disapproved. On the lower rostrum of his Tabernacle the open baptistry witnessed to one of the cardinal beliefs of his denomination.

Today most Baptist churches celebrate Communion or the Lord's Supper twice monthly--the first Sunday evening and the third Sunday morning of each month. Yet as a denomination we claim to be scriptural. In Scripture we read that "on the first day of the week the disciples came together" to pray, to preach and to sing Psalms and hymns and spiritual songs, but Scripture goes on--to break bread. Every Lord's Day the early Christians met together to remember the Lord's death upon the cross. Had they not been told "Do this often?" Spurgeon was an advocate of the weekly observance of the Lord's Table. He believed the New Testament set out only two ordinances, both commands of the Lord, and we should observe them according to His Word.

What a sight it must have been each Sunday. The ground floor area and the first gallery both filled with communicants. Several hundred more stayed in various parts of the building as spectators. Twenty-three elders broke the loaves and served the vast crowd with orderliness and reverence. No wonder many testified to becoming Christians through remaining as spectators.

Spurgeon said he was "strict" as regards membership, that is, that all members should be baptized before being received into membership, but he was "open" as regards the Lord's Table, that is, that all, baptized or unbaptized, so long as they were believers, were welcome at the Lord's Table. Let his own words, reprinted in his magazine from a Communion meditation, provide us with his convictions about the two ordinances.

> The outward ordinances of the Christian religion are but two, and those two are exceedingly simple, yet neither of them has escaped human alteration; and, alas! much mischief has been wrought, and much of precious teaching has been sacrificed by these miserable perversions. For instance, the ordinance of baptism as it was administered by the apostles betokened the burial of the believer with Christ and his rising with his Lord into newness of life. Men must needs exchange immersion for sprinkling and the intelligent believer for an unconscious child, and so the ordinance is slain.

> The other sacred institution, the Lord's Supper, like believers' baptism, is simplicity itself. It consists of bread broken and wine poured out; these viands being eaten and drunk at a festival--a delightful picture of the sufferings of Christ for us and of the fellowship which the

saints have with one another and with Him. But this ordinance, also, has been tampered with by men. By some the wine has been taken away altogether or reserved only for a priestly caste, and the simple bread has been changed into a consecrated host. As for the table, the very emblem of fellowship in all nations--for what expresses fellowship better than surrounding a table and eating and drinking together?--this, forsooth, must be put away, and an altar must be erected, and the bread and wine which were to help us to remember the Lord Jesus are changed into an "unbloody sacrifice," and so the whole thing becomes an unscriptural celebration instead of a holy institution for fellowship.

Let us be warned by these mistakes of others never either to add to or take from the word of God so much as a single jot or tittle. Keep upon the foundation of the Scriptures, and you stand safely and have an answer for those who question you, yea, and an answer which you may render at the bar of God; but once allow your own whim, or fancy, or taste or your notion of what is proper and right to rule you instead of the word of God, and you have entered upon a dangerous course, and unless the grace of God prevent, boundless mischief may ensue. The Bible is our standard authority--none may turn from it. The wise man in the Proverbs said,"I counsel thee to keep the King's commandment;" we would repeat his advice and add to it the sage precept of the mother of our Lord, at Cana, when she said, "Whatsoever He saith unto you, do it."

We shall now ask you in contemplation to gaze upon the first celebration of the Lord's Supper. You perceive at once that there was no altar in that large upper room. There was a table, a table with bread and wine upon it, but no altar. And Jesus did not kneel--there is no sign of that,but he sat down, I doubt not after the Oriental mode of sitting, that is to say, by a partial reclining--he sat down with his apostles. Now, He who ordained this Supper knew how it ought to be observed, and as the first celebration of it was the model for all others, we may be assured that the right way of coming to this communion is to assemble around a table and to sit or recline while we eat and drink together of bread and wine in remembrance of our Lord. (1873, 61)

## The Hymns and Music

Visitors to the Tabernacle for the first time were often impressed by the prayers of the preacher rather than his sermon. They were also greatly blessed by the hearty singing of 6,000 voices. Yet Spurgeon did not believe in organs or church choirs. The note to sing by was sounded by a precentor with his tuning fork.

Although it is apocryphal to say that Spurgeon described a choir as "the war department of the church," he certainly disliked them. That, however, did not prevent him from enjoying visiting choirs during the week. For instance he wrote in his "Notes" that "the Jubilee Singers had a grand reception at the Tabernacle, every inch of available space being occupied, and hundreds turned away from the doors for want of room." (1873, 429) He went on to describe the occasion:

The melodies which in the bad old times were the favourites of the poor slaves were rendered by our emancipated friends in a manner altogether unique; we have never heard anything like it; it was pure nature untrammeled by rule pouring forth its notes as freely as the wild birds in spring. The people were charmed . . . Wherever they go we hope they will obtain a hearty welcome. (Ibid)

In the same way, although he agreed with the Scots that organs were "a bag of wind" not suitable for the worship of God, he gave away two silver trumpets to two of his evangelists for use in the services.

Of organs he wrote:

We heartily agree with Dr. Glasgow and should like to see

all the pipes of the organs in our Nonconformist places of worship either ripped open or compactly filled with concrete. The human voice is so transcendently superior to all that wind or strings can accomplish that it is a shame to degrade its harmony by association with blowing and scraping . . . That the great Lord cares to be praised by bellows we very gravely question; we cannot see any connection between the glory of God and sounds produced by machinery. (1874, 89)

In the same year, reviewing a book about *The Remarkable Musical Talents of Several Members of the Wesley Family*, he quoted Adam Clarke's representation of John Wesley's opinion of musical instruments in church:

"I have no objection to instruments of music in chapels, provided they are neither heard nor seen." Clarke added, "I say the same, though I think the expense of purchase had better be spared." (Ibid, 438)

In spite of Spurgeon's magazine giving the impression that he was entirely anti-music in church worship, he was large-hearted enough to allow others to hold the opposite view. As Bob L. Ross points out in his book, *Campbellites, Cow-Bells, Rosary Beads and Snake Handling*, Spurgeon remarked referring to musical instruments:

We . . . do not affirm them to be unlawful, and if any George Herbert or Martin Luther can worship God better by aid of well-tuned instruments, who shall gainsay their right?

And as Pastor Lennie Wilson points out, referring to Spurgeon's *The Bible and The Newspaper* (page 106):

Praise may be rendered with musical instruments, if you will; but the danger is lest the grateful adoration should evaporate, and nothing should remain but the sweet sounds.

It is also pointed out in Bob Ross' book that John Wesley did not oppose the use of instruments in worship, but the abuse thereof. (45-47) Adam Clarke, however, was clearly anti-instrument.

Book reviews are also a mine of information as to Spurgeon's thoughts about various hymns. Reviewing *The Augustine Hymn-book* Spurgeon commented:

> It must be confessed that too many so-called hymns are more fitted for groaning than singing and ought never to be offered for the use of an assembly of believers although they may be very well suited to individual cases of mournful experience. (1866, 140)

To counteract all his criticisms he brought out his own collection that same year entitled *A Collection of Psalms and Hymns for Public, Social, and Private Worship* (Ibid, 474), *Our Own Hymn-book* as it came to be called. Yet he acknowledged later that the hymn book for Sunday schools had not yet been compiled:

> The hymnology of youth is yet in an unsatisfactory state; much has been done; more is doing, but the materials are not yet extant for such a hymn-book as would be worthy of the Sunday-schools of England. (1869, 478)

Thus the *Golden Bells* or *Hymns for our Children* by the Children's Special Service Mission (later the Scripture Union) came under fire:

> We think the committee have attempted too much; for we are not sure of the wisdom of issuing so large a book for children ... We are surprised to find the book contains so large a proportion of hymns from *Songs and Solos* (Sankey's hymn book): it is hardly fair to that publication.

He did not really like Sankey's music. He acknowledged that the book had done "great service to the good cause" (1882, 495), but he had already stated five years previously:

> Already the hymns and tunes made popular by Mr. Sankey are falling into disuse in our schools and chapels--a few only being sung at prayer-meetings. (1877, 137)

It just goes to show that C. H. Spurgeon was not infallible in all things as some biographers seem to imply, for *Golden Bells* and *Songs and Solos* have both had a considerably longer run than he prophesied.

As for the modern hymns, modern in his days, Spurgeon could have been speaking in our own twentieth century. At the time of his writing for his magazine there was a move on foot to discredit and depreciate the hymns of Isaac Watts, some even proposing that some, if not all be set aside. Spurgeon rebuked the anti-Watts brigade with the words:

> This treatment of Watts is an ungrateful suggestion, and if it does not betray a dislike to the evangelical tone and the frequent doctrinal statements of his hymns, it certainly betrays exceeding narrowness, if not shallowness or judgment in the matter of poetry. (1890, 362)

Seven years before he had criticized a collection of hymns containing much new and fresh material although they had been put together by two of his own evangelists. Spurgeon's trenchant comment could have been for much present-day material published in the variety of modern hymn-books offered to churches.

> They will get along for another year or two, and perhaps by that time the church will be wise enough to come back to our grand old Psalms and hymns and the music of our childhood. (1883, 509)

Regarding hymns for the Communion Service he was very decisive:

> We should not choose a tune for the communion table which is not very soft. These are no boisterous themes with which we have to deal when we tarry here. A bleeding Saviour robed in a vesture dyed with blood-- this is a theme which you must treat with loving gentleness, for everything that is coarse is out of place. While the tune is soft, it must also be sweet . . . But oh! it must also be strong; there must be a full swell in my praise. (1867, 488)

No wonder there were hundreds of spectators at his weekly observance of the Lord's Supper. They were not only spectators but auditors--those influenced by the hearing ear as well as by the seeing eye.

## The Activities

There were many church activities that went on, Sundays and weekdays, in connection with the Tabernacle. Children, women, benevolent agencies, the training of pastors and preachers, tract distribution--and for all of them Spurgeon believed he had New Testament warrant.

We have here the rare instance of a Christian Church containing within itself all the varied appliances of Christian zeal in modern times. These have risen successively and expanded as the spontaneous and appropriate expression of that zeal. This may go far to show that it accords with apostolic times. If the principles and motives be the same, the fruits, allowing only for the difference of circumstances, will be the same. Nor is it difficult to see a similar diversity in the methods of aggression in the primitive Churches according to the circumstances of those times.

The Church at Jerusalem had its mission both to the Jews and to the heathen. There it was, says Paul, that "James, Peter, and John gave to me and Barnabas the right hand of fellowship; that we should go unto the heathen, and they unto the circumcision."

The Church at Antioch had its foreign mission, for it sent forth Paul and Barnabas on a missionary tour into Asia Minor. "When they had fasted and prayed, and laid their hands on them, they sent them away."

They had their Pastor's Collegem, for Paul says to Timothy, "The things that thou hast heard of me among many witnesses, the same commit thou to faithful men, who shall be able to teach others also."

They had their Home Missions, for of the Church at

Thessalonica, it is said, "From you sounded out the word of the Lord in Macedonia and Achaia."

They had their Tract Societies, as far as circumstances would allow."When this epistle," said Paul to the Church at Colosse, "is read among you, cause that it be read also in the Church of the Laodiceans."

They had their Bible Classes. "There were more noble than those in Thessalonica, in that they received the word with all readiness of mind, and searched the Scriptures daily, whether those things were so."

There were Mrs. Barlett's classes in those times. "Help those women which laboured with me in the Gospel."

They and their Benevolent Societies. "It hath pleased them of Macedonia and Achaia to make a certain contribution for the poor saints which are at Jerusalem."

They had their working ladies for the poor. Honourable mention is made of one to show how honourable it is in all. "There was at Joppa a certain disciple named Tabitha, which by interpretation is called Dorcas: this woman was full of good works and almsdeeds which she did." We are then informed of what those alms-deeds conformed and of what those alms-deeds consisted. We should have supposed they consisted in money only; but no, she gave her time and her labour. At her death, "all the widows stood by Peter weeping, and showing the coats and garments which Dorcas made while she was with them."

If there were no Sunday Schools in the first Churches, it was simply because they had neither the learning nor the books required,--not even the Scriptures. A foundation was laid for them by the Master when He said, "Suffer the little children to come unto me, and forbid them not: for of such is the kingdom of heaven." Although, therefore, all the institutions connected with our Churches are of recent origin, the germs of them existed in primitive times and remained for development when that which hindereth should be taken out of the way. New as they may be in practice, they are not new in principle or theory.

They are the natural growth of true Church principles which struggle for expansion by every legitimate means and on every side. Remove the pressure of outward violence and inward formality, and the Church springs up to this as to its natural state and breathes its native air. It is by the great variety of aggressive means that the zeal and efforts of each and all the members of our Churches are brought to bear upon the same end. It enables every one to answer the question for himself, "Lord, what wilt thou have me to do? (1865, 175)

Such a Church with its many agencies in incessant operation becomes a power, not in this country merely, but also in the world. Such were the first Churches in Corinth, in Phillippi, in Ephesus and in Rome. Most of these arose, as in the case before us, almost entirely from the labours of one man. Is not this then, we ask, as we appeal to its efficiency, as we appeal to its spirituality, as we appeal to its internal harmony, as we appeal to its development of all Christian gifts and graces, and as we appeal to its freedom from all the evils of secular ecclesiasticism--Is not this the fashion after which the Gospel was originally designed to spread and in which it can best be extended into any country and in any age?

Such a catalogue of church activities, supported as they are by New Testament counterparts, might well form the basis for discussion today especially among Reformed churches who often take the view that the church is a family and should worship together at all times, not hiving off into different activities. Even the well-tried and tested Sunday School movement is shunned. Spurgeon, an avowed Calvinist, saw that different organizations within the church not only had New Testament support but showed the way to New Testament success.

# CHAPTER FIVE

# Anglicanism and Catholicism

Before the first issue of *The Sword and the Trowel* in 1865, Spurgeon had preached and subsequently printed his sermon on baptismal regeneration. That was followed by an article on the "Nonconformists Burial Bill" in *The Baptist Magazine* in 1861. In it he expressed his love for all evangelicals in the Anglican Church yet "blushing" for their inconsistency in remaining in it. He rejoiced that many of them were protesting against the Papists and Infidels in their midst (the Puseyites and Essayists) but felt they should come out of such a system that was supported and upheld by the State. Spurgeon firmly believed in the Disestablishment of the Church of England.

> He was even more strongly opposed to Catholicism, referring to the Roman Catholic Church as "the Popish Antichrist." Men of all religions and no religion should deprecate the growth of a system which rendered the Inquisition possible. (1868, 341)

For Spurgeon, the Popery in the Roman Catholic Church was just the same as Popery in the Established Church. He denounced it in both camps through writing articles, reviewing books and publishing tracts (complete with etchings of High Churchmen dressed up like Roman Catholic priests). The tracts were called *Sword and Trowel Tracts*, printed in the magazine and also as separate leaflets for distribution. (e.g. 1865, 357)

Naturally he got into hot water from some members of the Establishment for reproducing such pictures of clergymen in what he called "fancy dress." He offered no apology, since "like a cold bath early in the morning, (the shock) will do them good." He reaffirmed his decision to publish such literature, "We are not going to handle the abominations of the present Anglican establishment with kid gloves." (1868, 468)

WHO is this gentleman? You guess him to be a Romish priest; and so indeed he is, but he is not honest enough to avow it. This, with the exception of the face, is a correct representation of a clerical gentleman, well known in the south of England, as a notorious clergyman of that religious association, which is commonly, but erroneously, called "The Church of England." We can assure the reader that our artist has faithfully given the robes and other paraphernalia with which this person makes a guy of himself. We beg to ask, what difference there is between this style and the genuine Popish cut? We might surely quite as well have a *bona fide* priest at once, with all the certificates of the Vatican! There seems to be an unlimited license for papistical persons to do as they please in the Anglican Establishment. How long are these abominations to be borne with, and how far are they yet to be carried?

Protestant Dissenters, how can you so often truckle to a Church which is assuming the rags of the old harlot more and more openly every day? Alliance with true believers is one thing, but union with a Popish sect is quite another. Be not ye partakers with them. Protestantism owed much to you in past ages, will you not now raise your voice and show the ignorant and the priest-ridden the tendencies of all these mummeries, and the detestable errors of the Romish Church and of its Anglican sister.

Evangelical Churchmen, lovers of the Lord Jesus, how long will you remain in alliance with the defilements of High Churchism? You are mainly responsible for all the Popery of your Church, for you are its salt and its stay. Your brethren in Christ cannot but wonder how it is that you can remain where you are. You know better. You are children of light, and yet you aid and abet a system by which darkness is scattered all over the land. Beware, lest you be found in union with Antichrist, when the Lord cometh in his glory. What a future would be yours if you would shake yourselves from your alliance with Papists and semi-Papists. Come out for Christ's sake. Be ye separate, touch not the unclean thing!

He wrote about disestablishment right from the second volume of The Sword and the Trowel:

> To the very principle of a State Church we are constantly opposed, and to that form of it which is seen in the Anglican Establishment we have the further objection that it is the nurse and propagator of Popery. (1866, 418)

And in the same volume: "However evangelical the Church of England may become, it will never be able to compete with Dissenting churches either in piety or usefulness until it gives due honour and scope to what it has been pleased to call lay agency." (Ibid, 428) Today, of course, the Church of England is making more and more use of lay ministry so the reader must judge whether this is due to Spurgeon or to enlightenment from the Scriptures.

In a review of *The Religious Objections to the Union of Church and State* he begins by commending the book as "a first-rate piece of artillery against the abominable union of Church and State . . . Every Dissenter should buy two copies--one for himself and one to give away to his nearest Church of England neighbour. (1867, 284)

He had no time for Bishops as is evidenced in an article entitled "Bishops! Bishops!" in his magazine. He began by saying:

> If Bishops be, as certain ecclesiastics appear to think, the panacea for all the ills of the church, the church in London ought to be in the soundest condition, for the town swarms with bishops as Egypt once swarmed with frogs. English, Scotch, Irish, Colonial, American, all varieties are abundant... Dr. Watts asks the youthful catechumen, "Can you tell me, child, who made you?" Now, your grace of Oxford, Nassau, Quebec, Graham's Town, never mind which, can you tell me who made you? Who anointed you to be lords where Jesus says that all are brethren?" (Ibid, 468)

There was one Bishop he did commend, however. Reviewing a book called *A Sermon Under the Sky*, a sermon preached in the open air in Seven Dials, St. Giles, he wrote:

The Bishop of St. Giles more completely discharges the duty of his seer than any other episcopus in the land; and the manner of his ministry is such as to prove him a more genuine successor of the apostles than any mitred gentleman on the bench. (1868, 331)

Taken to task by an Anglican clergyman for overlooking all the good in the Church of England, he replied, "So far from doing so, we are perhaps as well acquainted with the good side of Anglicanism as our critic himself. We most unfeignedly rejoice to see clergymen evangelical and wish they were all so to the fullest extent; the Evangelical party in the Establishment is the only one with which we can hold the least spiritual brotherhood; at the same time, we cannot cease from expressing our regret that enlightened ministers should remain in fellowship with a church in which rationalists and Papists find so appropriate a home and should profess to agree with a prayer-book which teaches baptismal regeneration as plainly as words can speak. (1869, 41)

Reviewing a book by the Prebendary of St. Paul's Cathedral he said that when reaching page twelve he "smelt a strong smell of Roman candles." After reading of baptismal regeneration, fonts and altars he began to sniff again "for there was a remarkable odour of abounding plagiarism" (reminiscent of Paxton Hood's lectures on Lamps, Pitchers, and Trumpets). The result was that he "pitched the book to the other end of the room" and cried out, "Dead robbery!" He picked up the book with its back broken and muttered, "Served it right!" (Ibid, 93).

Spurgeon was a personal member of The Society for Liberating Religion from State Patronage and Control. And so he believed that "the State, as such, ought neither to patronize nor persecute religion." (1870, 330) In spite of that he paid tribute to the Ecclesiastical Commissioners who "agreed with great courtesy to sell the freehold" of the ground they owned on which the Pastors' College was built. "As we often hear of instances of refusal to sell to Dissenters on the part of the great ones of the earth, it is only right to let it be known that the conduct of the Ecclesiastical Commissioners to us has been all that could be desired." (1877, 91)

But four years before he had advised people not to vote, if they were Nonconformists, for the Liberals or the Tories, if those parties would not aid in the disestablishment of the Anglican church. His chief reason was:

> (While) full-blown Popery is restored to her pulpits, we are bound to demand that this shall no longer be the national church. (1873, 476)

Reviewing a book of *Protestant Hymns and Songs for the Million* (the review is interesting for the depth of feeling there was against High Church ritualism), Spurgeon delighted in quoting one of the "hymns" in full. One verse is ample to illustrate Spurgeon's "We hope the rogues will enjoy it:"

> Incense, vestments, tapers,
> Bowings, crossings, bells,
> Pantomimic capers,
> Dark Monastic cells,
> Everlasting masses,
> Morning, noon, and night;
> Monks who dress like asses,
> Nuns in black and white!

This is hardly the kind of doggerel designed to win friends and influence people let alone bring back the ritualist from the error of his ways. Yet Spurgeon in his review suggested that boys and girls "learn them by heart, and sing them up and down the streets." (1874, 40)

Accused soon afterwards by a critic of his attitude towards the ritualists, his accuser stating that "there is not much likeness between us and the monk who brought Christianity to England," Spurgeon assured him that "there is no similarity, for all that his blessed monk did was to force Popery upon a nation." (Ibid, 341)

Disestablishment for Spurgeon would result in a purification of ecclesiastical language. In a review of a book dealing with transubstantiation the author, clergyman explained the derivation of "priest". Spurgeon asked,

What sense does it convey to the people? If the clergy mean to call themselves presbyters or elders why not do so, and we shall understand them, but so long as they call themselves priests they will be understood in the Romish or pagan sense ... Will this misuse of language never end? Never till disestablishment takes away the cause of all this stuttering and stammering, not to say equivocating and shuffling. (1875, 449)

Mariolatry, with its use of objectionable prayer-language, was also anathema to Spurgeon. *The Mother of Jesus not the Papal Mary* was published by the Wesleyan Conference Office and highlighted Mariolatry in the Established Church. It had Spurgeon's approval, being "one of the ablest exposures ... we have ever seen." Since "the worship of the virgin is becoming common in the English Church" and such prayers as "Holy Mary, mother of God, intercede for us" were being used, he wondered where it would all end. Spurgeon asked, "How can (it) end while the motley crew who man our Established Church find themselves able to eat the bread of a Protestant nation and teach as much of Popish idolatry as they please? If they must have their Maries, let them pay for them with their own money, but to tax us for this abomination is tyranny. (1875, 544)

In the same way he objected to Sacramental Confession in the Church of England when viewing a book of that title. "It is a thing not to be pruned, but unrooted." (1876, 40) In his "Notes" he mentioned the Burials' Bill upholding the right "to bury our dead in the graveyards which belong to every Englishman." (Ibid, 285) And the consecration of banners, flags, ships of war, etc. by the Established Church he looked upon as "a crying evil, dragging as it does the name of the Prince of Peace into connection with instruments for shedding blood and the insignia of carnage ... God has given no authority to any man to do any such acts in His name. (Ibid, 330)

He saw the Established Church as a great waste of national property and money. In his monthly "Notes" he described a city church in which one Sunday there were nine in the congregation and twelve performers: minister and clerk, six choristers, organist, blower, beadle and verger ... some city congregations are not quite so crowded. (1878, 318)

There were exceptions, however. How he rejoiced to receive for review the book *Holy Footprints*. "At first we thought he must be a Baptist, but we were compelled to read the title page . . . 'Vicar of St. Mary's, Hastings'."

Spurgeon reviewed the book with enthusiasm:

Fancy a man who practices infant sprinkling speaking and writing thus: "He calleth unto Him. Not first to the church, but to Himself. Not first unto the waters of baptism, but to Jesus. Not first to ordinances, or ceremonies, denominations or unions, but to a crucified and living Saviour . . . Jesus first--Jesus only. All the others are good only when He is first.' When we hear a vicar talk so we feel inclined to stamp our foot on this poor earth and say with Galileo, 'It moves.'" (1883, 512)

A comment made about another book might well have applied to the author of *Holy Footprints*:

How a simple faith in Christ can live and flourish in connection with forms and ceremonies of which the New Testament knows nothing remains a mystery to us. (1884, 602)

Some men did leave the Establishment and Spurgeon was glad to review a book by one who did so: *Why I am now A Baptist: Reasons for leaving the Church of England.* (1891, 193)

When all is said and done, however, the question has to be asked, Did all this written protest accomplish much? Did it cause Spurgeon and others a great deal of distress for nothing? In 1870 he dared to prophesy:

We need not fear that we shall endanger the crown rights of Jesus by unanimously resolving to break the bonds of the State from off the neck of every church now subject to it. Let Establishment men rage as they may; the evil is dead in Ireland, is dying in Scotland and shall be slain in England--God helping us. (1870, 285)

Now, over 120 years later the church of England is not

disestablished; they still have priests (even female ones) who dress from "Aaron's wardrobe" (as Spurgeon once called it) and who still have a Blessed Virgin Society and practice baptismal regeneration--even the evangelicals. So was Spurgeon's protest all in vain?

## Roman Catholicism

The Church of Rome was not exactly a different matter for Spurgeon, for he was continually pointing out the Romeward tendencies of the Anglican Church. There may not have been the evil of disestablishment in Roman Catholicism for Spurgeon to attack, but there were plenty of other evils for him to draw to the attention of his readers: the power of the Jesuits, the threat to civil liberties, idols, confessionals and rituals. He especially disliked the title "saint" given to people like Augustine, but even more so to Peter and Paul. (1875, 400)

He once lost one of his members to the Roman Catholic church, but he knew of only one. By contrast "we have baptized many Catholics who have not only escaped from the errors of their former creed but are most decided and established believers in the doctrines of grace." (1877, iii)

He also recorded an incident about an English lady in danger at sea in a small boat in the Mediterranean. She was rescued by a Roman Catholic fisherman who later visited her in her hotel in France and told her that he had the New Testament in English, French and Italian and "he had read Mr. Spurgeon's sermons." (1884, 94)

When exposing the errors of Anglicanism he received a letter from a clergyman telling him that his gout was a judgment from God for opposing the Church of England. What then could he expect as judgment for pointing out the errors of Roman Catholicism? "If a swollen leg proved that a man is under God's displeasure, what would a broken neck prove? . . . the amount of bitterness which the post has brought us during the last month has proved to our satisfaction that our blows have not missed the mark." (1874, 34f, 342)

In this twentieth century we are told that Rome has changed.

The effect of the charismatic movement upon Catholics, the wider availability of modern translations of the Bible, the joining in of Catholics at grass-root level with local interchurch activities--all these are offered as proof of the changing face of Rome. It was the same in Spurgeon's day. He was sent a book to review entitled *English Medieval Romanism*, "the design (being) to show what Romanism now is by what it once was."

Spurgeon once wrote:

> Romanism everywhere and at all times is essentially the same. It can put on different appearances, indeed, according to times and circumstances, but that is one of its essential characteristics. Its claims are unaltered, and it has never disavowed any of its former principles and decrees. (1873, 474)

Spurgeon's chief proof of the system's unchangeableness was the Jesuits or "the secret society" as it was referred to in a book he reviewed in 1873. He referred to them as

> Wickedness clothed in the garb of piety, more infernal than human, and, therefore, its works are in the dark. If anyone would know what part it has taken in the history of Europe; if he would know how far the Fenian movements in the United States and in Ireland, how far the late Ecumenical Council in Rome, and how far the recent wars upon the Continent, have been influenced by it; if he would know what its purposes and operations in this country are at the present time, let him avail himself of this [book] ...it is a **burning** as well as a **shining** light. (Ibid, 44)

Having given a lecture at the Tabernacle on Roman Catholicism he wrote afterwards in his magazine:

> The hand of the Jesuit is clearly to be seen in the mode in which our lecture on Rome has been assailed... A large number of newspaper writers are Papists, and to these the cue was given to represent the lecture as a burlesque. Half an eye will enable the reader to detect the cloven foot. (1872, 94)

In a six-and-a-half page article on "Jesuitism and the Jesuits" in his magazine he sets forth the influence and power of this secret society:

> The organs of Romanism in this country unblushingly avow their purpose, which is to crush religious and civil liberty.
>
> At first the pope restricted the numbers of the Jesuits to sixty, but the restriction was subsequently removed in consequence of the services rendered to the papacy. They then increased rapidly, and, guided by Loyola, soon overspread the nations, their great object being to reduce Protestantism to servile submission to the papal throne... Nothing could exceed their skillful subtlety. They sought the education of the young and became their sole teachers. They aspired to educate kings and queens and succeeded in becoming their priestly confessors. Every plausible pretence was used to gain over the minds of statesmen and men who wielded authority, and their good fortune was remarkable... The testimony of Pope Alexander VII is sufficient to prove what he termed 'the unbridled licentiousness' of their doctrines.
>
> England has always been the object of their desires. The conquest of this country to Rome has been a dream which Jesuitism has striven hard to make a reality.
>
> And these men have found their most invaluable allies in a church that boasts of being the bulwark against Romanism--we had almost written Protestantism: for the Anglican Church has now become the worst foe to the Gospel of Jesus Christ. If any one doubts this, let him read the current High Church literature where he will find men openly advocating . . . reunion with Rome. (1870, 301ff)

Through receiving many books to review from America Spurgeon was always *au fait* with what went on there in the American Christian world. By reading *Rome in America*, published in New York, Spurgeon was able to inform his magazine readers of the "heinous superstitions and hypocrisies of the Papacy." He ended his brief review with a personal prayer: "We wish that Old England and New England might both be rid of this plague. Such a volume as this may yet prove a ram's horn to bring down some of the walls of Romanism. God grant, this is our earnest prayer. (1884, 605)

His prayer for the end of Rome's influence in the world has not been answered any more than the one he uttered for the Church of England to become disestablished. Over one hundred twenty years later the Church of England is still looking towards unity with Rome. While her archbishops not only have an audience with the Pope but also pray with him; while Rome still denies their Communion Table to Protestants (and still refer to them as "separated brethren"); while they refuse to recognize the validity of their orders, their marriages, and much else besides, the prayers and protests and prayers must continue. The prayers of all Protestant believers are invaluable, but where is there a Spurgeonic voice that will be effectual in these days--even using twentieth century means of communication?

Note: There are so many references to Anglicanism and popery, High Church ritualism, and disestablishment that only a small number could be used in this chapter. The research student might like to look up the following extra references if he can gain access to copies of *The Sword and the Trowel*: 1865, 110 & 505; 1868, 227 & 332; 1869, 93 & 120; 1870, 92; 1872, 84; 1873, 566; 1877, 329; 1880, 352; 1885, 601; 1886, 42; 1887, 633; 1890, 192 & 203.

**CHAPTER SIX**

# Denominations and Isolation

An American writer once accused Charles Haddon Spurgeon of forming a network or distinct body of "Spurgeon followers." This new "denomination" was said to be composed of young preachers from his Pastors' College and the churches in which they were serving. The writer saw the time when Spurgeon would found a sect, following the example of John Wesley. Mr. M. Coit Tyler of America called it Spurgeonism.

Replying to the charge Spurgeon wrote in *The Sword and the Trowel*:

> There is no word in the world so hateful to our heart as that word "Spurgeonism", and no thought further from our soul than that of forming a new sect... We love Christ better than a sect and truth better than a party, and so far we are not denominational, but we are in open union with the Baptists for the very reason that we cannot endure isolation. (1866, 138)

Thus there are many references in his monthly magazine to the various denominations (some commendatory and some condemnatory) and also to isolationists like the original Plymouth Brethren.

### Congregationalists

Having been brought up among the Congregationalists (Independents) he was somewhat surprised to find that he had upset them in an article he wrote in *The Signs of the Times*. It appears they took exception to his outspoken views on the baptism of believers by immersion.

In his "Notes" in *The Sword and the Trowel* he said:

We are somewhat surprised at this, for they are generally well informed upon most matters and might therefore have known the views of Baptists. We have said no more than we and our brother Baptists have always believed... We have spoken plainly, and mean to do so still; we have cherished the most brotherly feelings towards all Paedobaptist friends and shall do so still; we do not ask them to conceal their distinctive views, and we certainly shall not conceal ours; ours is the charity which neither padlocks another man's tongue nor consents to hold her own. (1873, 568)

## Methodists

He had more to write about Methodists for they were a larger denomination, and he also greatly admired the Wesleys--once giving a lecture at the Tabernacle entitled "The Two Wesleys."

In 1870 Spurgeon reviewed as a separate article in *The Sword and the Trowel* a book about John Wesley by An Old Methodist, a former Methodist turned High Churchman, a renegade who had become a violent partisan according to Charles Haddon Spurgeon. He had become a priest and "therefore set himself with evident delight to the work of converting his former comrades from the error of their ways."

Spurgeon set himself to the task of defending Wesley against the false charges made against him by the Old Methodist. Wesley was not a ritualist as the "Old Methodist" made out. True, he was "greatly influenced by the manners of the country whence he came out." Thus Wesley believed in Baptismal Regeneration, mixing water with the wine at the Communion (Spurgeon quotes from Wesley's works to prove this), but he was a firm believer in Justification by Faith. (1870, 120ff)

A similar theme occupied the mind of Dr. J. H. Rigg who wrote a book entitled *The Churchmanship of John Wesley*. Spurgeon reviewed it and praised the author for a "trenchant and powerful little volume" that showed "how intense and real was Wesley's revolt against Anglicanism." (1880, 82)

In the same way he was able to commend the author of *Methodistic Ritualism*, a work by "an Old-Fashioned Methodist" showing up the current errors to be found in that denomination: the "natural goodness of children," the "non-necessity of conversion for children of pious parents," being two of the more serious errors. Spurgeon rejoiced "to see a champion for the faith raised up among our Methodist friends," acknowledging that "there is a gospel which we hold in common, and we grieve when we see the slightest sign of apostasy from it." (1885, 600)

*Golden Candlesticks* or *Sketches of the Rise of some early Methodist Churches* by John Bond received a much more favourable review. "A book fitted to thrill the souls," wrote Spurgeon. He continued, "Would Ritualism defile this unhappy land if we were as zealous as the old Methodists? We trow not... If all other Christian denominations will follow in the same hearty enthusiastic style of service, a grand day will come for England."

He appreciated the book so much that he commented, "We hardly know where to make an extract, it is all so good." In the end he quoted a lengthy portrait of a Methodist hero--Thomas Lee, a preacher who suffered terrible persecution and at the end of his life exclaimed, "Lord, if Thou wilt, give me strength, I will begin again." (1873, 564)

Another favourable review is of great interest since it was a book written by a Methodist minister who was trained at Spurgeon's Pastor's College. The Rev. Danzy Sheen became a Primitive Methodist minister "of great repute and usefulness" and was "one of the alumni of our college." Spurgeon had been following his career with interest and took "great delight in his prosperity and growing talent." His book was entitled *Shiloh*, but we are given no evidence of its subject matter--only that it was "spiritual and edifying, the style pleasing and flowing. (1870, 138)

But Spurgeon's real admiration of the Methodists was for their system of class-meetings. He was always happy to review books about them and commend them to others. *Thoughts about Class-Meetings: a series of Letters to an Enquirer from a Methodist Pastor* was well-reviewed and the class-meeting system described as "the strength of Methodism" and "a pretty general adoption of the system in all our churches would be a very great blessing" guarding people against "the insidious errors of the day." He saw no Scriptural warrant for making attendance at the meetings a condition of membership but did see in God's Word "much which requires us to provide frequent meetings for mutual edification." (1869, 330)

One author did see that attendance at the meetings should be a condition of membership. Reviewing his book Spurgeon once again advocated the system but was against it being a condition of membership, calling such a thing "tyranny" and if insisted upon would be a "deadly wound of Methodism." (1868, 564)

Perhaps Spurgeon's greatest tribute to the Methodist denomination was when the president of the Wesleyan Conference died in 1865. W. L. Thornton, MA was only fifty-five years of age but was a "distinguished preacher, a tutor, and an editor of a magazine." Spurgeon told the readers of his magazine that he looked "with sympathy upon this denominational bereavement. Though differing in sentiment upon certain points in theology of considerable import, we cannot withhold our grateful acknowledgment of the extensive usefulness of the Wesleyan Methodists in all parts of this land, and our unqualified admiration of the self-denying zeal of many of their ministers." (1865, 179)

## Quakers

Spurgeon had a great regard for the Quakers or Society of Friends, especially for George Fox (1624-1691), the English founder of the Society. Charles Haddon Spurgeon would have approved of Fox's denunciation of the evils to be found in certain churches, clergymen, and especially soldiers.

When in 1876 the Baptist Union meetings were held in Birmingham some leading Baptist ministers were invited to breakfast by the then Mayor of Birmingham. He happened to be a member of the Society of Friends, and they were so impressed by his Christian witness and testimony that some said, "If I were not a Baptist I must become a Quaker." Spurgeon commented, "We believe this to be the general feeling--certainly it is ours."

The Friends do not observe the two ordinances which was plainly unscriptural for Spurgeon, but when they become "saving ordinances" or "in any way contributing to salvation," then he could understand the Quakers being driven to reject the outward symbols altogether. (1876, 529)

Some years before those Baptist Union meetings in Birmingham Spurgeon had written an article, "Among the Quakers," in his magazine. He put out feelers about his speaking to the Society. He felt called of God "to arouse that most respectable community to greater energy and zeal." He wanted them to renew their earlier testimony against formalism, ritualism and unspiritual worship. Although he confessed, "Our doctrinal views widely differ," he said that they were one when standing out against those important evils.

He continued,

> After the lapse of some months a door of utterance was opened, and... with very great thankfulness, but bowed down under our responsibility, we found ourselves in the midst of a most cordial company of about twelve hundred Friends in their meeting-house at Bishops-gate Street... Although suffering much physical pain, it was one of the happiest seasons of our life when we stood up in the crowded assembly to speak for Jesus to those who love his name.
>
> Our object was not to moot points of difference but to stimulate brethren to strive for those precious things wherein we agree. We did not feel that we had any right to controvert, nor indeed does our spirit move in that direction; we felt full of love to the Lord's living people and desired in tenderness and humbleness of mind to exhort them to more fervour and boldness.
>
> Oh that the Holy Ghost may seal our testimony! It was delivered with great solemnity of soul and was attended with many cries to God; surely it will not be in vain. We only wanted one thing more, viz., the permission to have poured out our soul in prayer upon the spot, but as our esteemed friend, Mr. Gilpin, seemed to indicate that

silence would be preferable, we did not feel at liberty to do so. However, there was much heart-prayer in the assembly, and we humbly but eagerly look for results. (1866, 554)

It was well-reported in the Quakers' newspaper, *The Friend*, and Spurgeon himself published the full address through his usual channels, Messrs. Passmore and Alabaster.

In *The Friend* it was described as "a message of mercy from the Almighty." Like Spurgeon, he was disappointed that vocal prayer was not uttered, for "the work of the Spirit upon or in the heart should be left unfettered." The writer hoped that Spurgeon would pay them another visit, and that he would, on such an occasion, be "left at liberty to do his Master's work in his own way." (Ibid, 555)

## *Isolation*

### The Plymouth Brethren

Spurgeon would not recognize the Christian Brethren of today. No longer are they the Plymouth Sect of his day. The only body he would recognize would be the "exclusives." The Open Brethren, some now charismatic, some having family services in the morning and the breaking of bread service in the evening (he maintained all along that our Lord instituted a Supper and not a breakfast), some having full-time pastors, especially on the mission field where church buildings with a cross adorning the outside rather than a simply unadorned gospel hall. They have a representative on the organizing committee of the Women's World Day of Prayer, which comes under the auspices of the World Council of Churches. Many have full-time workers in this country that are virtually pastors who meet with their local ministers' fraternal.

No, Spurgeon's Plymouth Brethren were the original "Darbyites" who majored on eschatology, bringing down upon their heads his famous remark, "Ye men of Plymouth, why stand ye gazing up into heaven."

They had no time for denominations, and besides being practicers of separation, they also lived in isolation. They were very severe in their criticism of Spurgeon, as he was of them. If they did not regard themselves as a sect, then Charles Haddon Spurgeon did.

> They tell us with the utmost persistency that they are not a sect; what they are then is left to our conjectures, and we have thought that it must be interpreted in one of three ways. If they are not a sect, they may pretend to be the Church of Christ on earth--holy, catholic and undivided. This, we think, is really too absurd to need refutation. Or perhaps they are not a sect because, attached to no particular fellowship, they holy communion with all who love the Lord Jesus Christ, in whatever denomination they may be folded together.
>
> That such however is not the case; we have palpable evidence, for their adherents are the most captious, quarrelsome, cynical and exclusive professors of religion to be found among Protestants. What other solution of the riddle can we fly to unless it be that they are not a sect or section of the church of Christ at all? This view has been recently taken in the adjudication of one of our law-courts and so far as we can discern in simple justice without any breach of charity. What palpable element of a church can you discover in a divided fraternity which acknowledges no creed, no ministry, no church order, substitutes private meetings for public worship, owns no rule as to one ordinance and gives a social rather than a sacred character to the other ordinance? We sincerely hold that their identity is not positive enough to be determined, and their profession too saponaceous for us to take hold of. (1866, 371 & 372)

Why should Spurgeon have been so hard and critical of them? Was it just because of their peculiar doctrines or their palpable divisions? No, Spurgeon had, in fact, suffered similar criticism and even persecution at their hands. For some time they had been giving tracts to people entering the doors of his Tabernacle. He considered it almost beneath his notice to answer something that was so "devoid of all sense, Scripture and reason," but he did speak out in his magazine that in the eyes of the Plymouth Brethren "the unpardonable sin is declared to be speaking against the Darbyites." He likened them to "the infallible gentleman who occupies the Vatican!" This was after one Darbyite "industriously spread the tidings that Mr. Spurgeon is a blasphemer."

In his article in *The Sword and the Trowel*, Spurgeon affirmed that his "name and character (were) in too good a keeping to be injured by these dastardly anonymous attacks." He held Mr. Newton and Mr. Muller in high regards and did not believe that they sanctioned such attacks upon him.

Spurgeon concluded, "It is worthy of note that even the printer was ashamed or afraid to put his name to the printed paper!" (1867, 32)

Particular doctrines and interpretation of Scripture that he took exception to were, first of all, their definition of "the church." According to them "it is the actual living unity with Christ and with each other of those who, since Christ's resurrection, are formed into this unity by the Holy Ghost come down from heaven."

Not so, according to Spurgeon, for "the bride has not her counterpart on this earth. While Christ, who is our life, is absent, the life of the saints is hidden--hid with Christ in God. The New Jerusalem is out of sight. The Epiphany of the church is a feast yet to be celebrated." (1867, 121 & 122)

Spurgeon also refuted their claim that the Old Testament saints do not belong to the church (in a review of one of their pamphlets). The Brethren argument was that "Christ did not exist as the Bridegroom before his ascension," but according to Charles Haddon Spurgeon "both John the Baptist and our Lord himself tell us the reverse." (1866, 565)

They even went so far as to state that "Old Testament saints have no part in the promise to reign with Christ in glory." He replied that their "empty conceit of their own superiority has led to displace Abraham, Isaac, and Jacob, together with all the saints of whom Moses said, in the name of the Lord, 'All his saints are in thy hand.'" (1866, 371)

Not only was their doctrine of the church wrong, according to Spurgeon, but also their views of worship. Reviewing *The Brethren*, their worship and the Word of God at open variance, Spurgeon recommended this "capital pamphlet for distributing where Plymouths are working after their manner." He commended the pamphlet's author, Dr. R. H. Carson, for drawing attention to "their ecclesiastical history" which becomes "more and more sorrowful, for it is a reproduction of the divisions and contentions which other bodies have had to deplore." (1881, 575)

Their disunity was highlighted in Scotland in a book which Spurgeon reviewed. Spurgeon was delighted with the book, exclaiming, "Solid Presbyterian brethren make short work of P. B. whimsies by bringing down the sledge-hammer of Scripture upon them." He acknowledged that when they began "no people began with higher aims or nobler prospects, but none have failed so egregiously... They are the body, who, above all others, have preached unity, and exhibited to the world a spectacle of disunion, bickerings and schism among themselves and of unparalleled bitterness and bigotry towards other bodies of believers." (1874, 388)

One of their founders, E. K. Groves, wrote *Conversation on 'Bethesda' Family Matters* and Spurgeon reviewed it thus: "Family matters are not to be talked of in the street, and dirty linen should be washed at home." Referring to the Exclusives, he said, "Their ecclesiastical system is more worthy of Rome than of Zion, and its history reads more like a record of the doings of the order of Jesuits than account of the acts of a Church of Jesus. The work commenced by brethren Muller and Craik was a living one, and it lives still. Let us think more of this God-given success than of the blunders of those who went from them and beyond them... May the gracious Head of the Church preserve us from the repetition of those ferocious deeds of unbrotherly schism which have been wrought in the name of unsectarianism!" (1885, 596)

Not only was it the Exclusives' exclusiveness that disturbed Spurgeon but their inconsistency. Reviewing a book by Edward Dennett, *The Plymouth Brethren: the Rise, Divisions, Practice and Doctrines*, he stated,

Here are facts, which among all men of Christian character and intelligence, will brand the Darbyite system with richly-merited condemnation. There was much of good in the early Plymouth movements, and the churches are none the worse for what they learned from it, but the cloven hoof soon appeared, and the good was speedily over-balanced by the evil. Never surely in any age or place have more glaring inconsistencies been perpetuated in the name of Christianity, or more sectarian principles been promulgated under the pretence of unity." (1870, 382)

He always rejoiced when others openly found fault with the Darby system so that he alone was not firing the bullets. He once thanked the Bishop of Sunderland (and he loved bishops!) for "so seasonable and sensible a deliverance" when reviewing the Bishop's "Friendly Letter to the Christians called 'Brethren,' on the Subject of the Ministry." He summed up the "Friendly Letter" in these few words, wishing he had more space to give it in his magazine:

Very friendly, certainly, but very forcible too, and as we conceive, very crushing. The arrogance of Brethrenism, as developed in some quarters, needs just such faithful rebukes as this tractate affords. (1869, 43)

Two things really saddened him about the Exclusives or "Close" Brethren. First their faulty Biblical interpretation. Reviewing Mrs. Machlachlan's *Notes on the Parables*, according to literal and futurist principles of interpretation, he described them as

Oracular and dogmatical in the highest degree and about as far-fetched as the comments of Origin. When we reached a point at which the authoress feels it needful to warn us that the gospels are Jewish in their teaching, we judged it time to have done. Systems of interpretation which find it necessary to depreciate inspired books give very clear evidence that their origin is not from above. (1873, 523)

Yet he was saddened by a movement that began well, had

a great deal to teach the denominational churches and then developed into a system marred by all the faults which he felt bound to point out in *The Sword and the Trowel*. He summed up these feelings of sadness when reviewing in that magazine a reprint from *The British Weekly*--"Life Among the Close Brethren."

He commented,

> In their earlier days (they) bore grand witness for the truth of God, and they aimed at a high ideal of church life. Fidelity to the Word of God was their eminent characteristic. They were hindered by none of the fashions of the day or the customs of the churches in carrying out their resolve to stand alone in the ways of the Lord rather than yield a hair's breadth to human policy.
>
> Among them were some of the excellent of the earth, well-instructed saints, far-seeing students of the Word. But an evil spirit came in. One brother became the virtual head of the community, and at his bidding true saints of God were cast out, and a sect was formed which may challenge all others for extreme exclusiveness... We do not sympathize with the spirit which can take pleasure in this exposé, but we hope it may act as a warning to godly men. (1891, 249)

The subsequent history of the Exclusives, since the death of Spurgeon, has surely proved the accuracy of his criticisms. May it prove, in the prayerful words of Spurgeon, "a warning to godly men."

## CHAPTER SEVEN

# Rupture and Censure

Having seen what Charles Haddon Spurgeon thought about other denominations, what did he think about his own, and in particular the Baptist Union? Many people, thanks to the rather doubtful details given in biographies (especially present-day ones), think that Spurgeon was always against the Union. Others sum up his attitude by saying that 'he didn't beat the Baptist drum, but he didn't kick it either!'

Such is far from the truth. The Down-Grade Controversy* or the interpretations of it that we are given in books, magazines and doctoral theses seem to imply that Spurgeon was always anti-Union. The truth is very different. He held the Union in high regard for a great many years, frequently preaching for it at their annual meetings. It was only in 1887 that things came to a head and prepared the way for a rupture between Spurgeon and the Union, to be followed by their censure of him.

Before the rupture there had been rumblings, many of them over-looked by biographers because they failed to research the volumes of *The Sword and the Trowel*. Before we look at and listen to these, and before we outline briefly what the controversy was all about, let us notice the love Spurgeon had for his fellow Baptists.

As early as 1866 he was writing in his magazine:

The gatherings of our brethren in Liverpool were unspeakably delightful... Nothing could exceed the cordial spirit of brotherly love which reigned among us. There was about the whole affair a life of loving earnestness, which augured the happiest future for the Baptist body... By God's grace we are banded together to build up for

---

* *The Down-Grade Controversy*, published by Pilgrim Publications, contains Spurgeon's public materials on this issue.

the Lord Jesus a firm bulwark for the defence of the truth. (1866, 521)

Even one year before the Down-Grade storm broke he wrote with great charity:

These papers (read at the Autumnal Session of the Baptist Union in 1886 and reviewed in his magazine) are all good. We should like every Christian man in the world to study this (the Rev. Charles Williams') address. We take it as a prophecy of brighter days for the Baptist Union, for the future lies with those Christians who will keep to purity of doctrine and of life. (1887, 40)

In between he had written:

The meetings of the Baptist Union have been held at Manchester, and... it is pleasing to observe the growing union and force of the denomination, and it is to be hoped that no difference will ever arise. (1872, 530)

And five years later:

It (the May meetings) was as happy and enthusiastic a feast of brotherly love as could be well looked for this side heaven; the Baptists are no longer a heap of units; we are coming together, cohering and uniting in one, and in all this ultimate designs of God for the spread of His truth are manifesting themselves. Never were the signs more hopeful. God is with us, and the whole brotherhood feels the value and need of that presence. We see everywhere the true evangelic spirit, in happy contrast with other quarters where intellect is idolized and novelty of doctrine sought after. (1877, 284)

But six years later he is making a strong protest about the "sayings and doings" of the Baptists Union meetings in Leicester:

I, for one, have no Christian fellowship with those who reject the gospel of our Lord Jesus Christ, neither will I pretend to have any... There is a point beyond which association may not be carried, lest it become a confederacy in disloyalty. This point can be speedily reached, if it be not felt by all that the unwritten law of the Baptist Union takes it for granted that its members adhere to those grand evangelical truths which are the common heritage of the Church. We cannot remain in union on any other basis... There can be no real union among Baptists unless in heart and soul we all cling to the Lord Jesus as our God, our Sacrifice, and our Exemplar. We must be one in a hearty love to the gospel of His grace, or our unity will be of little worth. It is my own personal belief that no number of men under heaven are heartier in love to Christ crucified, and to one another, than the great majority of our brethren of the Union: with them I am heartily at one, and in writing these lines I fear lest I may cause them pain; but I can say no less if I am to bear a conscience void of offence towards God. I may only add that these lines are not written without much careful thought and earnest prayer. God grant that they may for the present suffice as a protest, not for myself alone, but for the many who share my anxiety. (1883, 607 & 608)

That the mild protest did not suffice is clear from his stronger protest made five years later. It all hinged on the doctrine of "future probation." Many of the Union's members avowed it, but a great number "rejected it... (as) a stranger among Baptists." Spurgeon expected some to begin preaching purgatory and praying prayers for the dead. He did not want to see "would-be trials for heresy," for he believed they did more harm than good. What he wanted the Union to do was to "tell the world what it believed." He could not trust the present council to do that, for they might "say one thing and mean another." He himself was looking for "a gracious revival as the true antidote for the new unbelief."

Some months later he appealed in his magazine "Notes" for much prayer to be offered on behalf of the forthcoming annual meetings of the Union. The great question before them would be: "Is this Union to have an Evangelical basis or not?" Since "every other body of Christians avows its faith, the Baptist Union should do the same... Should the majority decide that there shall be no Evangelical basis, the conflict will then begin... We have come to the parting of the ways, and the old school and the new cannot go much further in company--nor ought they to do so. Let them part with as little friction as possible. (1888, 197 & 198)

For his part he was issuing a pamphlet entitled, "Creed or no Creed? A question for the Baptist Union." The penny pamphlet was being written "by the brother who first wrote on The Down-Grade."

Several biographers of Charles Haddon Spurgeon, even present-day ones, have suggested that the "brother" Spurgeon referred to was either Spurgeon himself, writing anonymously, or the Rev. Robert Shindler. If only they had done their research into the volumes of *The Sword and the Trowel*, they would have discovered the truth. The first of the articles appeared in the 1887 volume, the month of March, and the second the next year (August).

In 1892, after Spurgeon's death, R. Shindler was writing in the July issue of *The Sword and the Trowel* on "Mr. Spurgeon's Early and Later Ministry." In it he said, "The preliminary papers on the Down-Grade tendency of modern thought, which *I wrote at his suggestion* (author's italics), and which, in their utter want of judgment, some attributed to his own pen, opened the way for his own powerful, effective, and faithful utterances. (1891, 420)

The articles may have "opened the way," but Spurgeon had, like a signpost, pointed out the road the Baptist Union and others had been going for some many years. Right from the first volume of *The Sword and the Trowel*, in articles (his own and those of others he asked to contribute) and in book reviews (a rich but much-neglected source of information), he pointed out the liberalism or modern-thought as he sometimes called it that was creeping in among the various denominations, and especially the ministers.

In 1865, therefore, when reviewing a book called *The Duration of Future Punishment* he commended it for speaking out against "the annihilation heresy." Many seem to think that eternal condemnation versus annihilation only appeared on the scene at the time of the Down-Grade controversy. But in his review

Spurgeon emphasized that "these lectures will, we trust, put many in possession of the antidote to the poison which is so zealously distributed. (1865, 466)

That Spurgeon was right then, and during the Down-Grade, is proved by the way some prominent evangelicals are preaching the same doctrine today.

The following year another review, *Forever and Ever: the Duration of Future Punishment*, contained this forceful statement by Spurgeon:

> The doctrine of the eternity of future punishment might in itself appear to be of minor importance, but it holds such a position in the Christian system that its denial or doubt almost necessarily leads to error upon all the other truths or revelation. (1866, 382)

Four years later in his "Memoranda" column he defines the doctrine, as he understood it, more clearly:

> We do not look upon the mere endless existence of souls either as punishment or a reward; it pleased the Lord to make them immortal, and they are now such of necessity; their reward is not eternal existence, neither is their punishment eternal existence; unending existence is theirs as souls, be they bad or good. The reward of life in Christ Jesus never to our mind could be confounded with existence; it has a far higher, more spiritual and divine meaning; it is sacrilegious to pull it down to so grovelling a sense. The punishment of everlasting destruction is also to our apprehension a very different thing from utter annihilation; it is such a destruction as an everlasting thing is capable of. The continued existence of the wicked is not their punishment, their punishment lies in the wrath of God, which has fallen upon them, as the natural effect of sin. (1870, 190)

The following year he commended a book on the *Eternal Suffering of the Wicked* as "calculated to give rest to the minds of those who are tossed about by modern opinions," (1871, 332) so modern thought was perceived by Spurgeon some sixteen years before the public controversy of the Down-Grade. In the intervening years we get book review after book review highlighting this false doctrine that was to become a burning issue in 1887 and 1888. In 1872, *An Enquiry into the Eternal Punishment of the Wicked* was reviewed and the story told with great glee of men in a public house saying, "Mr._____ is the parson for us. He won't send us to hell forever for our sins." And so they "continued to indulge in their drunkenness and wickedness."

With deep regret he discovered that "the Congregationalists appear to be straying from the old orthodoxies. One of them informs us that the wicked will be annihilated and another that they be ultimately restored... our own intention is to labour with all our might to save men from everlasting punishment." (1874, 341) The same year he commended a commentary by Dr. Meyer because it was helping to counteract the "modernism" and "skepticism" of German scholars "who have much to answer for." (Ibid, 580) Later he commended a *Reply to Supernatural Religion*, a book which "showed how the influence of German and anti-Christian literature can be withstood and neutralized. (1875, 236)

Two years later he became more outspoken in the Preface to the annual volume of *The Sword and the Trowel*:

> We know a denomination in England which is sadly gangrened with a pseudo-intellectualism which counts it manly to doubt, and reckons the believer in the orthodox faith to be a weak-minded creature, worthy of their sublime pity. If this goes on, the prospect for those who indulge therein is none of the brightest; their fine notions will alienate the people and make many feel that even superstition is better than cold negations and the chill of perpetual questioning. Where this modern thought comes, it is the hand of death, and all things which are worth preserving wither before it... never did it more prevail than now. Never had we a firmer hope or a brighter expectancy. (1877, iv)

How wrong he was in those closing words--it was only a decade before the debacle highlighted by the Down-Grade Controversy. *Modernism* gained momentum:

The rationalistic treatment of the Old Testament records by such critics as De Wethe, Davidson, and Ewald... the profanities of [their] "Higher Criticism"--these needed answering by evangelical scholars; (1878, 462) a well-nigh "complete refutation" of faulty doctrine about future punishment was commended in the same year; (Ibid, 508) and a "complete and elaborate treatise" on the subject of eternal punishment (entitled *Forever*) recommended some months later. Several theologians opposed to the doctrine were "weighed in the balances of Scripture and of reason," and "found wanting." (Ibid, 555)

*Everlasting Punishment not Everlasting Pain* received a bad review a year later because it was based on the "instincts of humanity" instead of the "infallible standard of Scripture" and therefore was "as feeble as it is fallacious." (1879, 539) Modernism was castigated the following year--the "follies of the Germans and the skepticism of the modern thought school" being exposed in a book entitled *Transcendentalism* which Spurgeon reviewed. (1880, 187)

So the laxity of evangelical doctrine continued to be shown up. The "restoration" school of theologians was derided next, those who believed that the vilest sinners would eventually enter heaven after a period of punishment. A "pompous little book" (*Sin and its Penalty, Present and Future*) was relegated to the scrap heap because Spurgeon believed that God did not "send us into the world to tell men that, unless they accept the gospel, they will be lost, and all the while had a backstairs to heaven by way of a bastard purgatory." (1881, 90)

The march of Modernism that year was highlighted in a review of *The Higher Criticism and the Bible*, which "loose German theorizing has led to unsettlement." Higher Criticism was denounced for "frittering away the force of the Bible by attacks upon its inspiration and genuineness." (Ibid, 235) Later "inspiration" was to be another cause of the Down-Grade protest. John's gospel "is the chief point of attack by the German school of destructive criticism," (Ibid, 289) he declared after reading and reviewing *The Creed of the Gospel of St. John* by an anonymous author.

*Evolution* was also a bone of contention in the Down-Grade controversy. Several years before things came to a head Spurgeon had defined his own position to Darwinism: "We look upon evolution as a questionable hypothesis. It is not yet an ascertained or acknowledged truth of science, and assuredly the time has not come to incorporate it with our faith in revelation." (1884, 88) He made the statement because a certain W. Smyth "as a preacher of the gospel in the streets and halls of Maidstone, has been for many years in the habit of introducing evolution into his evangelistic work, blending Scripture and Spencer in his addresses." The same man had just published a pamphlet which Spurgeon was reviewing: *Evolution Explained and Compared with the Bible*.

In a short article with the strange title of "Windmills or Butter-Pats" Spurgeon poked fun at the evolutionists of his day "who are unable to receive the Bible account of the creation." For himself it was sufficient that he "could believe what is revealed; for, sublime as it is, there is a kind of truth-likeness about it; but we cannot believe what we are now taught with such tremendous authority; for, in the first place, it is not worth believing, and in the next place, it looks so dreadfully like a lie that we had rather not." (1885, 349)

He was a staunch opponent of "Universalism," which was to be another error exposed during the Down-Grade Controversy. In the preface to his annual volume of *The Sword and the Trowel* in that same year, he stated:

> We see comparatively little of overt atheism, deism, or honest infidelity; but we are surrounded by men who subscribe our creeds and hate them, employ our terms and attach false meanings to them, and even use our pulpits as places of vantage from which to assail the vital verities of our faith. The latest fashion of this unbelief is Universalism... This deadly evil had its day in America, and it blighted every church it touched; the same result will follow in our own land if the disease should ever be widely spread. (1885, iii)

In the year prior to the first of the Shindler Down-Grade

articles Spurgeon once more poured scorn on Darwinism:

> We have no liking for attempts to reconcile [evolution] with the Bible, or the Bible with it. There is no need for reconciliation. It will be time enough to do this when the fanciful hypothesis becomes associated in some remote degree with facts. At present this madness is best left to its own ravings. (1886, 552)

Thus after quietly protesting since 1865 in his magazine, an anonymous writer (later to be known as R. Shindler) took up the cudgels on his behalf. The first article was in March and the second in April 1887. Each had an Editor's note urging that they be read with "earnest attention" for "we are going down hill at break-neck speed" and "the growing evil demands the attention of all who desire the prosperity of the church of God."

In his preface to the volume, written, of course, after it was completed, he wrote:

> What havoc false doctrine is making no tongue can tell. Assuredly the New Theology can do no good towards God or man... if it were preached for a thousand years by all the most earnest men of the school, it would never renew a soul... We look down into the abyss of error, and it almost makes our head swim to think of the perilous descent."

Recipients of the magazine were soon writing to the editor in support or with questions to be answered. Spurgeon was happy to write in his "Notes":

> We are glad that the article upon The Down Grade has excited notice. It is not intended to be an attack on any one, but to be a warning to all. (1887, 195)

It should be remembered that Spurgeon was not the one to bring named personalities into the controversy. The names were supplied by the other side, Mr. Booth, secretary of the Baptist Union. Spurgeon refused to name names.

He continued in the same "Notes":

> We are asked whether Methodists are upon the Down-Grade, and we are happy to reply that we do not think

so. In our fellowship with Methodists of all grades we have found them firmly adhering to those great evangelical doctrines for which we contend." How sad he would be today to see the Down-Grade of not only the Methodists but all the major denominations.

He went on to define the details of the Down-Grade:

Our warfare is with men who are giving up the atoning sacrifice, denying the inspiration of Holy Scripture, and casting slurs upon justification by faith. The present struggle is not a debate upon the question of Calvinism or Arminianism, but of the truth of God versus the inventions of men. All who believe the gospel should unite against that 'modern thought' which is the deadly enemy. (Ibid, 195 & 196)

Soon support was being given Spurgeon by the religious press and various churches and Baptist Associations. (see 1887, 511ff) These were collected and printed in an article entitle "The Case Proved." This was followed by another article called "A Fragment upon the Down-Grade Controversy." In it he dealt with the question of starting a new denomination--"not a question for which we have any liking. There are denominations enough. If there were a new denomination formed, the thieves and robbers who have entered other "gardens walled round" would climb into this also, and so nothing would be gained. Besides, the expedient is not needed among churches which are each self-governing and self-determining; such churches can find their own affinities without difficulty and can keep their coasts clear of invaders. (Ibid, 560)

Not everyone took the controversy seriously. A group of ministers thought it "a huge joke" as they talked about it on the train that was taking them to the Baptist Assembly being held at Sheffield. Thus Spurgeon included an article in *The Sword and the Trowel* entitled "The Down-Grade Joke." It had been written by Dr. R. F. Weymouth, headmaster of the public school at Mill Hill, Outer London, and translator of the New Testament into modern speech, a forerunner of those by R. Knox, J. B. Phillips, etc. "Those of us who share Mr. Spurgeon's views," wrote the good Doctor, for which support Spurgeon was most grateful. (Ibid, 561ff)

Even the Strict Baptists, the Hyper-Calvinists, supported his protest and sent him a signed resolution. (Ibid, 598)

Once more, in December of that fatal year he stressed that the controversy was not about Calvinism v. Arminianism, for he was supported by many of the latter in his stand for the truth. That was a "red herring" according to Spurgeon, the real issue being the "eternal verities--those foundation truths which are common to all believers which belong not exclusively to this party or that." It was a protest that gave him "great content of conscience" and was against those "who treat the Bible as waste paper, and regard the death of Christ as no substitution." (Ibid, 642)

The new year (1888) began with the confession that the controversy had "lost [him] many a friend" but, thankfully, his philanthropic agencies such as the Orphanage, had not suffered but rather gained financially. (1888, iii)

With what was later to be proved false optimism, he looked to the new year as being a time when "a drag has been put upon the Down-Grade wheel... hindering the deplorable advance of ruin." (Ibid)

In January his college men expressed sympathy with him in his protest. He did not expect them, however, to do as he did. Whatever they decided regarding the Union it would not "imperil our hearty union with each other. One by leaving, and another by remaining, may both be aiming at the same end." That was only for the time being. If things worsened ,and "it be once definitely decided that Universalists, rejectors of the Atonement, and persons who do not regard Holy Scripture as the infallible authority in doctrine are to remain in the Union, then it will not be an open question. The duty of Christian men will surely then be clear enough." (1888, 44)

The next month, R. Shindler, added more fuel to the fire by an article called "Are these Things so? or the New Theology." He emphasized Purgatory, Future Probation, Universalism, and described how the Down-Grade was affecting the Congregationalist church of America.

Taking up Shindler's points Charles Haddon Spurgeon affirmed in his "Notes" that the Baptist Union needed to draw up a resolution in which it rejected future probation and restoration as both unscriptural and unprotestant. If they did not do so, "we may expect to hear a full-blown purgatory preached, and prayers for the dead will follow as a matter of course." Not that he wanted to see "would-be trials for heresy;" if definite doctrines were laid down, "men who honestly differ will go" and the Baptist Union "could readily clear itself without going into personal details. Let it tell the world what it believes." (Ibid, 91)

A spate of books and pamphlets were by now being published and reviewed in the magazine. In *Outspoken* Spurgeon agreed with the author's "denunciations of the formalism, worldliness, and hypocrisy of the present age;" in *The Triumph of Modern Thought; or the Bible and how we got rid of it* he saw the need to rouse others "to fight in the battle for life itself which is now upon us;" "one of the few on the Baptist Council who can see things as they are" wrote *The Spirit of the New Theology*; poems by Newman Hall were reviewed, and though he was more of a liturgist than Spurgeon would ever be, Charles Haddon Spurgeon wrote: "he loves the gospel, and therefore we can forget his gown and prayer-book... he remains true to the cross" when all around "modern thought is poisoning the air." (Ibid, 138ff)

By now the controversy was gathering speed and support; "so it ought to do; for every one who follows it will see how every week the evil which we pointed out is more and more manifest." If he, Spurgeon, pointed it out, then it was more than just Shindler's articles, as we have already seen. "We have directed special attention to the post-mortem salvation and purgatory heresies... openly avowed; but other errors are also rife enough... It was time that some one spoke... this matter should be taken up by those churches and ministers that remain true to the old faith." (Ibid, 147) The matter to be taken up was the question of the Baptist Union formulating a Scriptural basis. He himself wrote to *The Baptist Times* and reprinted the letter in *The Sword and the Trowel*. (Ibid)

Sadness now crept in inspite of the support from all over the country. He was grieved to have to write, "The evil has affected some few of the men who were educated in our College... they have naturally found sympathizers, and this has been the sorest wound of all." He rejoiced, however, that others had written to him to say that they had been "recalled to more hearty preaching of the gospel, and aroused their people to more prayer. (Ibid)

He had by now withdrawn from the Baptist Union, and he printed a resolution (dated January 31, 1888) passed by the Tabernacle church meeting "endorsing his action... and pledging to support him by believing prayer and devoted service in his earnest contention for the faith once for all delivered to the saints." (Ibid, 148) This counteracted the rumours that the Tabernacle as a church was not in complete accord with its pastor. His hope now was that a period of calm faith in God would precede "a gracious revival of pure and undefiled religion." (Ibid, 149)

It was not the ministry alone that was affected by heresy. Spurgeon declared,

> It is... in the deaconship, and in the membership of the churches; not unbelief upon the outskirt truths, but upon the central teaching of revelation... In a few years' time, if the truth should again be to the front, it will scarcely be believed that one of the most pronounced bodies of Evangelical Dissenters hesitated to declare its faith. (Ibid, 249)

As time went by Spurgeon saw that the errors in the Baptist denomination were "ten times more widely spread than [he] knew of when [he] wrote the Down-Grade papers," and he did not feel he could "withdraw a syllable, but to emphasize each word with all our might." (Ibid)

After the Baptist Union re-elected the old council and passed a resolution that merely tried to "clear itself," Spurgeon was glad that he had resigned and "should never under any probable circumstances dream of returning... I have felt the power of the text, 'Come out from among them, and be ye separate,' and have quitted both Union and (London) Association once for all." (Ibid, 299)

Ungodliness was now causing him sorrow as was doctrinal

error. He had received complaints from magazine readers who had heard "sermons ridiculing answers to prayer, deriding early piety, speaking coarsely of the precious blood of Jesus and denying the universal need of conversion... certain preachers seem to have taken out a license to speak contemptuously of holy things, and they do this under cover of decrying the worn-out ideas of old-fashioned orthodoxy. Of course, they can do so with impunity when once their churches have become sufficiently worldly and heterodox." (Ibid, 378) One minister said to a brother pastor as they left a certain church, "There is truth after all in what Spurgeon says: ministers do make infidels, and this sermon will make a great many." (Ibid, 379)

A letter published in *Word and Work* was reproduced in *The Sword and the Trowel*. Written by Henry Varley, this "brotherly testimony" stated that "Separation, in my judgment, in Mr. Spurgeon's case, was wise and right. In no other way could he have made so effectual a protest." (Ibid, 446) So, too, "hosts of American friends have been at the Tabernacle and have greeted the preacher with loving sympathy. With these have come men of eminence and plain lovers of the gospel belonging to all denominations, bringing warm and tender words of sympathy and cheer." (Ibid, 515)

Canada, too, sent over their loving sympathy, passing a resolution at the annual meeting of the Baptist Convention. But by the end of the year the rupture was complete: "The Pastor and Church at the Tabernacle are now free from all hampering connections with Unions and Associations." (Ibid, 515) At the same time Spurgeon became a personal member of the Surrey and Middlesex Baptist Association, "agreeing in heart and soul with the members of it, it seems but natural to unite with them." (Ibid, 652) He still believed and prayed that a true revival, "a wind from the Spirit of God," would be "the surest method of blowing away the pestilential clouds of the Down-Grade." (Ibid, 653)

By the end of 1889 it was no longer just a Down-Grade among the Baptists and some Congregationalists in Britain and America, Spurgeon in "This must be a Soldiers' Battle" had to report:

> Scarcely a denomination is free from the enemies of the truth... In the Church of England the superstitious errorists

are more to the front than the skeptical... Among the Baptists, the great need is the personal investigation of the matters in debate by the members of our churches. It is clear that the members of the Council have nothing to say except by way of rebuke of any who protest against the growing error... A Congregational minister asks for an opportunity for the rank and file of the ministry to speak; and his impression is, that ninety-five per cent would be found to be on the old lines. We sincerely wish that we could believe it; but we think his percentage far too high... The Free Church of Scotland must, unhappily, be for the moment regarded as rushing to the front with its new theology, which is no theology, but an opposition to the Word of the Lord... Finding ourselves in a community which had no articles of faith, and seeing deadly errors rising up, we had no course but to withdraw. Whether others think fit to do so or not is no part of our responsibility. (1889, 633 & 634)

His somewhat pathetic confession just before the year closed was that "some of us who have been the first to discern the storm, have been made to feel an awful solitude from men, but a blessed communion with God." (Ibid, 651)

And on the final page of the magazine for 1889, in a book he wrote, "Judicial blindness has come to the teachers of the age: they have loved falsehood, and after it they will go. It is, however, the duty of every man, whatever the fashion of his mind, to speak out for the truth, whether men will hear or forbear." (Ibid, 658)

The new year began on a brighter note. Spurgeon could write in his preface: "The Down-Grade controversy has not been without benefit to the cause of truth. So far as we can judge, many ministers who were sliding downward have seen their danger, and are far more evangelical than they were." (1890, iii)

Once again various book reviews give an insight into Spurgeon's thoughts and opinions regarding the Down-Grade controversy. When reviewing a book, *On the Inspiration and Divine Authority of the Holy Scriptures*, he commends the author for putting forth "all his energies to defend the very foundation of it." This then presents Spurgeon with an opportunity to 'knock' those who "in this little day, in most of the churches, care two-pence for revealed truth" and at the same time fire a shot at the Baptist Union:

> "Save the Union!" is the one cry. "Glorify Nonconformity!" is the watchword. Oh, that the Lord would raise up a people of another mind, to whom truth would be precious, and the glory of God the one thing to be sought after! (Ibid, 36)

The eternal future was still a burning question with Charles Haddon Spurgeon. Giving a good review of *The Hereafter: Sheol, Hades, and Hell, The World to Come,* and *the Scripture Doctrine of Retribution according to the Law* he wrote:

> ...a fine book, and after our own heart. Those who have become unsettled as to the solemn question of the doom of the ungodly should get this book and study it. It deals crushing blows at conditional immortality, and the restoration theory; and we judge it to be a defence of the old faith which cannot easily be overthrown. (Ibid, 189)

The "sting in the tale" of a review of a book called *An Appeal to Unitarians* was:

> We have more hope of the conversion of an honest Unitarian than of the regeneration of those in our orthodox churches who profess to hold the truth and all the while hide away a lie in their right hand. These are legion. (Ibid, 536)

His autobiographical notes in the columns of his magazine again continue to throw further light on the Down-Grade Controversy. Answering a newspaper article that attempted to cheer him up out of his depression over the state of the churches, they said that "religion can never pass away." Spurgeon's reply in his "Notes" was:

> We never thought it could. No fear as to the ultimate victory of the truth of God ever disturbs our mind. We are

sure that the doctrines of the gospel will outlive the dotings of the 'modern thought.' The trouble is that, for the moment, error is having its own way in certain parts of the visible church, where better things once ruled; and, worse still, that good men will not see the evil, or, seeing it, wink at it, and imagine that it will do no very great harm. It is ours to give warning of a danger which to us is manifest and alarming; and if the warning makes us the butt of ridicule, we must bear it. Our protest is, no doubt, regarded by some as a piece of bigotry, and by others, as the dream of a nervous mind. (Ibid, 93)

Just as the newspaper correspondent used the word "depression" so the Americans were doubting his sanity. Asked what they thought of Spurgeon's conduct, several leaders of the Down-Grade informed their American cousins that "sickness and age had weakened his intellect." (Ibid)

The time had now come when preachers seeking another church were not "opposing any great doctrine, but dwelt upon matters which were true as far as they went." By leaving out the atonement, future punishment and the inspiration of Scripture they did not need to express their true beliefs about those doctrines. Churches had to take greater note "of what is not preached." (Ibid, 148)

On the other hand, he was informed by many that "when a Down-Grade teacher vacates his pulpit, the people very seldom have a desire for another of his class." Ministers who still held to the orthodox doctrines were closely associating with those who did not--"they can no more become one than oil and water... a compromise between truth and error is being maintained with great dexterity; but it is hollow as a drum." (Ibid, 460)

Besides false doctrines being preached he also stressed the down-grading in ministers' lives, especially in their attendance at theatre productions:

Those who denied the existence of Down-Grade tendencies took care to ignore one part of our charge-- namely, the down-going of the age towards worldliness. But if any have doubts on this point, let them think of clergy and ministers making up an audience for the play at Shaftesbury Theatre. Time was when such men would have found rebukers in their churches of the sternest order; but now they may go where they please, and only a few bigoted persons will criticize their conduct. (Ibid, 584)

Spurgeon had seen this coming, and warned about it, in two book reviews five and six years previous to the Down-Grade protest:

The modern theatre, which... even the daily papers which make no pretence of being religious, [confess] is growing more and more impure. How Christian men and women, above all how Christian ministers, can defend it we cannot tell. (1881, 288)

Well does our authoress confess her difficulty in writing about amusements for Christians, since no such word as amusement, recreation, game, or pastime can be found in the Scriptures. No: in the sacred book we read that time is short, and we bidden to redeem it. (1882, 35)

But back to the year 1890. In two articles, besides the book reviews and "Notes", Spurgeon had something important about the necessity of preaching faithfully the doctrines of grace and not succumbing to the modern thought of the Down-Grade. In Holding forth the Word of Life he said: "Our congregations are constantly plied with questions about inspiration, evolution, and progressive thought, our young people will become Unitarians first, and infidels afterwards, as surely as eggs are eggs" if the fundamental doctrines of the gospel "are kept back." (1890, 50)

"We must preach," he said, "the doctrines of grace more distinctly, and in more detail; gospel and water will not be sought after; but the genuine, and undiluted article will not want for admirers. Can we suppose that vast audiences would have imperilled their lives to listen to a 'modern thought' oration? Men are not so numerously insane." (Ibid, 51)

"The doctrines of grace," he declared, must be taught as carefully as if they were quite new, for new they will be to most minds nowadays. They have heard them caricatured, and wilfully belied; but they have never heard them expounded in their simplicity." (Ibid, 52)

In *Thoughts about Church Matters*, Spurgeon emphasized that his protest was not merely against one particular denomination (i.e. the Baptists):

> They have (not been so all along): our warning is for all Protestant churches alike; for though there be degrees of departure from the faith, and double-dealing with ecclesiastical terms may not in every sect be an equally flagrant fault, yet these evils are afflicting all the churches. The torrent of unbelief and worldliness rises above the hills, while it swamps the valleys. The duplicity which we denounce is not to be seen as a lone malignant star in one quarter of the heavens, but discerning eyes can detect its evil beams both in the northern, the southern, and the western sky. (Ibid, 212)

His discerning eye continued to see the down-grade trend even in the penultimate year of his earthly life, in spite of much physical suffering and absence from his beloved pulpit.

He continued to review books while on his sick bed. One was an important work by Professor Robert Watts of Edinburgh, *The New Apologetic; or, the Down-Grade in Criticism, Theology, and Science*. This was a book after Spurgeon's own heart, and he stated that "Dr. Watts meets the modern man with crushing argument, and exposes their sophistries mercilessly. But these gentleman are not moved by reasoning if based upon the Scriptures; neither does it seem as if the present race of professing Christians cared much about it either. Still, with the bare hope that candour may yet be discovered in workable quantities among the dupes of The Down-Grade, it would be very wise to introduce such a masterly work as this wherever an opportunity occurs. Right ideas of inspiration are defended, and the atonement is vindicated, while the whole of what is still known as 'orthodoxy' is maintained." (1891, 85)

In *Twenty Golden Candlesticks*, which he reviews with evident delight, he refers to the story in its pages about "a General Baptist Unitarian congregation, which certainly is not one of the Golden

Candlesticks." Looking into the future with his prophetic eye he comments:

> There will be plenty more of such congregations in the next generation if religious progress perseveres in its present direction, and if ministers become honest enough to avow themselves. They need not wear a mask nowadays; for if they believe anything or nothing, their denomination will still press them to its bosom, and aid them in deceiving the people. Mr. Doel's book affords many a warning against the Down-Grade, and many an encouragement for those who are true to their Lord. (Ibid, 339)

In reviewing a new volume in *Men of the Bible Series*, centered around Ezra and Nehemiah, he said of the latter: "More of [his] stern fidelity is greatly needed just now. If the churches would demand honesty in their preachers, they might not get it; but they might get rid of a set of cunning impostors who are just now ruling the roost." (Ibid, 457)

In his "Notes", he spoke out strongly about "the Church of the Future" and a Mr. Stead, who was posing as its leader, a friend of General Booth no less. He claimed to have "straight tips from God" that his futuristic church would include "atheists; run a theatre, and be the proprietor of a public house!" He was supported in this outrageous conception by the Rev. J. Clifford, ex-President of the Baptist Union. Spurgeon called such a church "grotesque, and defiant of Biblical teaching." He wrote that he had been bearing "our utmost testimony" against such a delusion. (Ibid, 93)

He also wrote against a Northern minister who had "glorified Mr. Bradlaugh (an MP)... as a man of true religion," yet he had denied the existence of God and spoken in the most violent manner against the faith, denying also the testimony of the Bible. (Ibid, 149)

He was still receiving letters of support, magazine readers writing to say that all he had said about the Down-Grade was true. Spurgeon emphasized that he did not speak "without knowledge. It was not possible for us to give up all our authorities nor would it have served any useful purpose to have published names; but we spoke truth which we could not help believing, and spoke it without exaggerating. Matters were even worse than we know of; if we had to bear our witness over again, we should not soften a syllable, but add emphasis to it. Indignant correspondents continually send us notices of amusements held by various churches; certainly they can hardly become more childish and inane. If we had a gracious revival, good people would find better things to do than get up [base] entertainments, and theatricals." (Ibid, 249)

That the sad state of affairs in the Union was getting worse rather than better is evident from a "Note" he made half-way through the year:

> The idea that loose theology is quitting the denomination is a fiction... The mischief lies at the door of Associations and Unions, which have allowed the poison to be spread, with something like their official stamp upon it. Ministers have quoted, with very slight censure, books which are ruining the souls of men, and the guilt lies at their door. It would be a great gain to the adherents of the old faith if they had a good weekly newspaper devoted to the cause. The other side has found much of its strength in periodical literature; it is remarkable that so little has been done in this direction by the orthodox. (Ibid, 348)

Thus we come to the last year of Spurgeon's earthly life and the 1892 volume of *The Sword and the Trowel*. In January he printed some *Sweet Experiences in 1842 and 1892*, but there was many a note of sadness rather than sweetness. As he saw the religious scene: "The churches are to a large degree making ready for the return of chaos and medieval darkness, the men who are sound themselves lie side by side with those who are rotten. (1892, 5)

While desperately ill at Menton in February, he wrote from his sick-bed:

> By this time we shall scarcely again be charged with wantonly raising the cry of "Wolf" without a cause, when we earnestly warned the churches that infidelity was

permeating the ministry. A fierce controversy is now raging, everywhere, over the inspiration of the Scriptures; and this is involving the Deity of our Lord, and indeed every other truth of Christianity. (Ibid, 92)

In a report of the Pastors' College Conference proceedings, the first following the death of their president, Charles Haddon Spurgeon, Mr. Harrald, Spurgeon's private secretary, gave a poignant message from Mrs. Susannah Spurgeon, concluding with these words:

> The Down-Graders cannot censure him now;
> he is far past all that!
> (Ibid, 315)

"Censure"the word means, according to the *Oxford Dictionary*, "an expression (official or authoritative) of disapproval or blame." Spurgeon's censure by the Baptist Union was then an official pronouncement and attitude by the council of that denominational body. By contrast the rupture that came about before the censure was the breaking off or "breach of harmonious relations" (*Oxford Dictionary*) by an individual between himself and that same official body of people. The dictionary goes further in defining "rupture" as "disagreement and parting." In other words the rupture came about because of Spurgeon's disagreement with the Baptist Union over doctrine and their failure to define publicly and in print their creed.

*The Sword and the Trowel* from 1865 to 1892 has provided us with twenty-eight years of autobiographical material showing Spurgeon's fears that such a Down-Grade was eventually inevitable. Three years after his death, when much of his previously unpublished material was being used by the successor to the editorial chair, a piece appeared in the February issue entitle "A Chapter of Autobiography." Spurgeon wrote it "nearly thirty years ago" according to the then editor of the magazine, and was "even more timely than we had anticipated." The article was written by Spurgeon at a time when he could only describe it as "the present hour is one of extreme peril... the mass of heathenism which crowds our great cities... the terrible indifference to divine things... Romanism... infidelity of the most cunning character... the rapid growth of Tractarianism... Popery... skeptics in canonicals!"

He asked the questions, "Is nothing to be done? Can nothing be attempted? Is there no demand made upon believers now to vindicate the truth? Are we tamely to sit still? Let a crusade against Puseyism and all other error be proclaimed, and let all faithful souls enlist in the great war. In the name of the Lord we will set up banners, and join in the fray."

## CHAPTER EIGHT

# Unity not Uniformity

Churches Together is not a new conception of church unity. There have been those who have dreamed of, and worked towards, visible unity among the denominations for many years. Even in Spurgeon's time the Congregationalists were trying to unite with another denominational body as they have succeeded in so doing in this twentieth century. But wherever there has been such a coming-together, there has always been a remnant who have refused to participate.

In his "Notes" for 1887, Spurgeon noted that while there were many crying out for unity "the main need of this age is not compromise, but conscientiousness... It is easy to cry 'a confederacy' but that union which is not based upon the truth of God is rather a conspiracy than a communion." (1887, 196)

Twenty years previously he had written an article for *The Sword and the Trowel* called "Ourselves and the Annexationists." He was concerned about the Congregationalists or Independents trying to increase their numbers by "offering facilities for transfer to its own ranks, and inaugurating a policy of annexation" which would be "unwise and unbrotherly." He thought that "to attempt to convert men to our views is our duty, but to draft them without conversion into our body is no gain in any sense, either to truth or good fellowship."

Thus he condemned a group who were trying to amalgamate Baptists and Congregationalists. This he described as "the thin end of the wedge--in plain Saxon, a little dodge." The result of such unity would be the forming of churches and founding a denomination "in which Christ's ordinance of baptism would be left optional; some of them would even have a font and a baptistry in each place of worship."

This was being done in some places, the resultant places of worship being called Union Churches. He called them "United Baptist and Unbaptized Congregationalism." He added, "There is one baptist at least who will never be absorbed into the projected unity!" That "one Baptist" would "quite as soon join the Free Church of Scotland, or the Quakers as the Congregationalists; but our anchor is down and not at all likely to be drawn up." (1867, 326ff)

Reviewing a book with the title, *Precious Ointment*; or the *Dew of Hermon on the mountains of Zion*, Spurgeon had this to say about visible unity among Christians of different denominations: " A special reservation in favour of his own church must inevitably frustrate the writer's design... The Church of England is the Church with which all Dissenters should be united, is the modest and conciliatory proposal as the basis of Christian unity." (1866, 333) That was the dew of Hermon on the mountains of Zion. Certainly Charles Haddon Spurgeon would not agree with our modern view of unity that "denomination," by changing the order of the letters, can read, Not Made in Zion!

Yet he would as much favour being "identified with the Church of England as with the Congregational Union, now that its members allow the grossest errors to be vented in its assemblies almost without protest." (1874, 341)

For Spurgeon the different denominations were but "various regiments formed in the one army," but "to break up the ranks in order to unite the army would be a foolish procedure." His advice was, "Let those who are united in Christ, and in His doctrine and ordinances, never dream of giving up their union with each other." All Christians should "cultivate abounding love to all the saints, even to those whom he judges to be in error upon certain points. Let him work with all believers as far as he can, but let him obey the ordinances of the Lord's house, and maintain the faith once delivered to the saints. To do this he will find it needful to join to the fullest degree with those like-minded." (1880, 582)

Although he never openly supported, or spoke for, the new holiness movements coming into being (the Keswick Convention, for instance), he would have agreed with their adopted motto that usually graced their platforms on a long banner: "All one in Christ Jesus." He was at one with all who believed the cardinal truths of the gospel. It did not matter if they were Calvinist or Arminian, Methodist or Quaker, Church of England or

Independent; he enjoyed fellowship with them because Christ was their common Saviour and Lord.

Reviewing a book entitled, *Church Unity: What is it?*, he said that he would not mind a pulpit exchange with a clergyman, but the fault was theirs if it did not come about. He praised a certain clergyman for inviting a Baptist brother to his church to read the prayers. He had done this as a protest because he, the clergyman, had wanted to attend a meeting in a Baptist church but was forbidden to do so by the local incumbent. "We like the brother's offer," said Spurgeon; "Shall we never see the end of this dis-union?" He welcomed the book on unity as "welcome as a drop of dew." (1886, 547)

Just before he died he had this to say about unity:

> During the past year I have been made to see that there is more love and unity among God's people than is generally believed... I had no idea that Christian people, of every church, would spontaneously and importunately plead for the prolonging of my life. I feel I am a debtor to all God's people on this earth. Each section of the church seemed to vie with all the rest in sending words of comfort to my wife and in presenting intercession to God on my behalf. If anyone had prophesied, twenty years ago, that a dissenting minister, and a very outspoken one, too, would be prayed for in many parish churches, and in Westminster Abbey and St. Paul's Cathedral, it would not have been believed; but it was so.
>
> There is more love in the hearts of Christian people than they know themselves. We mistake our divergences of judgment for differences of heart; but they are far from being the same thing. In these days of infidel criticism, believers of all sorts will be driven into sincere unity. For my part, I believe that all spiritual persons are already one. When our Lord prayed that His church might be one, His prayer was answered, and His true people are even now, in spirit and in truth, one in Him. Their different modes of external worship are as the furrows of a field; the field is none the less one because of the marks of the plough.

Between rationalism and faith there is an abyss immeasurable; but where there is faith in the Everlasting Father, faith in the Great Sacrifice, and faith in the Indwelling Spirit, there is a living, loving, and lasting union. (1892, 52)

It was while recuperating at Menton in the South of France that Spurgeon experienced some of the deepest spiritual unity with those of other denominations. He wrote in his "Notes" that Mr. Hudson Taylor has looked in upon us; Pasteur Bost we have also met both in public and private with great delight, and we have had most profitable and pleasing [fellowship] with the beloved George Muller, of Bristol." (1879, 193)

Sometimes this fellowship was enjoyed in the sitting room of his hotel; at other times it was at an informal breaking of bread service, meeting "with three or four, or twelve or twenty, as the case may be... There is no need to prepare a sermon, the bread and wine are text and discourse all ready to hand. Simple prayer, and suitable song, with the reading of the Word, make up a complete service, and requiring no laborious study, always preserving its freshness, and evermore bringing before our mind the most weighty of all themes." (1880, 151)

In his "Notes", just over a year prior to his death, he recorded that "each Sabbath the gathering at 'The breaking of bread' has consisted of members of all the churches, and of many nationalities." (1890, 92)

So much for those critics who said that the Down-Grade had made him an isolated, sad and lonely man. At Menton he enjoyed some of the richest Christian unity a man could wish for, and when he died in that much-loved Mediterranean resort, a Memorial Service was held in the Presbyterian Church there. There was now a gap or an empty chair in the circle of Christian friends representing several different denominations, all of them making up what was known as the Pastor's "Menton Circle."

## CHAPTER NINE

# Inspiration and Translation

In *Letting the Lion Loose: C. H. Spurgeon and the Bible*, it was pointed out that Spurgeon was like John Bunyan: "Prick him anywhere and he bleeds the Bible."* The main thrust of the book was to show how Charles Haddon Spurgeon saw such spiritual success in his ministry because that ministry was a sustained interpretation of God's Word. He preached **from** the Bible, he taught **about** the Bible, and he commented **on** the Bible. In *The Sword and the Trowel* we have many autobiographical passages that throw light on Spurgeon's attitude to the Word of God that are not to be discovered elsewhere. His concept and understanding of inspiration and also his thoughts and usage of various translations are to be found in the treasure chest of these twenty-seven volumes of his magazine. They also contain hints to believers on how to read and study and appreciate the Bible for themselves, as individuals and at family worship.

### Inspiration

The inspiration of God's Word, was of course, as we have already seen, one of the major points that he highlighted during the Down-Grade controversy. Long before the time of that controversy, however, Spurgeon made his own position clear in the third volume of *The Sword and the Trowel* in a review of a book upon the subject of inspiration--*God's Word Written: the Doctrine of the Inspiration of Holy Scripture Explained and Enforced*. The book was "an argument for verbal inspiration" and "worthy of the respectful attention of those who deny the doctrine."

As for himself he was able to say "That the Holy Scriptures

---

* *Letting the Lion Loose* by E. W. Hayden (Ambassador Productions, Belfast, 1984). Quotation from BBC television film, **The Calling of C. H. Spurgeon**.

were written by inspiration, and are an infallible statement of truth, is, however, a doctrine about which we, at least, have no difficulty." (1867, 43)

Ten years later he was able to state his unshakeable faith in God's Word once again. Reviewing A Treatise on the Inspiration of the Holy Scriptures he said, "It is upon the full verbal inspiration of the Bible that we cast anchor. We must have infallibility somewhere, and we find it here." (1877, 536)

He was always glad when he discovered others who believed in the inspiration of the Scriptures however much they differed on other points of doctrine. When Canon Liddon preached on it in St. Paul's Cathedral Spurgeon gave a lengthy extract in *The Sword and the Trowel* and added a footnote: "We are glad that this great preacher has such light upon the inspiration of the Scriptures. We differ widely on some important points, but in this we are at one." (1890, 168)

By contrast he took severely to task those who tried to undermine the verbal inspiration of God's Word. Reviewing *The Jewish People in the Times of Jesus*, he criticized it for stating that Luke in his gospel made erroneous statements, merely because there were no historical proofs. "For our part," wrote Spurgeon, "we shall believe in Luke's statements, whether they are confirmed or not... We believe the inspired evangelist in preference to everyone else. We will not endure... to be told that there are errors in the original gospels; and we feel indignant with Christian writers who insinuate that there may be... Nothing as yet has been proved against the accuracy of Biblical history, and we are sure that nothing ever will be." (1891, 196)

Inspiration and ethnology (the history of the races or nations) were compatible for Spurgeon. Reviewing *The Origin of Nations* in 1878, he condemned those who tried to prove that the antiquity of Egypt and Babylon were older than "is assigned to them in the Scriptures." Spurgeon commended the book under review for showing how "the ethnology of the Bible is shown to harmonize with all other historic records." (1878, 43)

If we want a definition of inspiration from Spurgeon's own pen then there are two important passages in his magazine. The shorter one is contained in a book review of *The Book of Proverbs*.

R. F. Horton, the author, was trying to distinguish between the inspired speech of a Biblical prophet or poet and the speech which was the product of human wisdom and observation, as if the latter was only inspired in a secondary sense. "We venture to think," wrote Spurgeon, "there is no warrant for this secondary use of the term inspiration. What is merely human is not inspired at all in any real sense. Where Scripture deals with records other than God's words or deeds, we are informed of the fact; as when Satan speaks, or the fool says in his heart, 'No God'." And so, for Spurgeon, the *Book of Proverbs* "was in the Jewish canon. They are among the 'all Scripture given by inspiration of God' to which our Lord gave his divine seal. Their subject-matter, and their authorship, may affect their style, but cannot touch their inspiration." (1891, 341)

What then, was Spurgeon's detailed explanation of verbal inspiration. He gives it in a fairly lengthy passage which must be quoted in its entirety:

### The Human Side of Inspiration

One might suppose that believers in Plenary Inspiration were all idiots; for their opponents are most benevolently anxious to remind them of facts which none but half-witted persons could ever forget. Over and over they cry, "But there is a human side to inspiration." Of course there is; there must be the man to be inspired as well as the God to inspire him. Whoever doubted this? The inference which is supposed to be inevitable is--that imperfection is, therefore, to be found in the Bible, since man is imperfect. But the inference is not true. God can come into the nearest union with manhood, and He can use men for His purposes, and yet their acts may not in the least degree stain His purposes with moral obliquity. Even so He can utter His thoughts by men, and those thoughts may not be in the least affected by the natural fallibility of man. When the illustration of the Incarnation is quoted, we remark upon it that the Godhead was not deprived of any of its moral attributes by its union with manhood; and even so, in the union of the divine and human in the inspired Word, the thoughts of God are in no degree perverted by being uttered in the words of men. The testimony of God, on the human as well as the divine side, is perfect and infallible; and however others may think of it, we shall not cease to believe in it with all our heart and soul. The Holy Spirit has made no mistake, either in history, physics, theology, or anything else. God is a greater scientist than any of those who assume that title. If the human side had tainted the lesser statements we could not be sure of the greater. A man who cannot be trusted as to pence is hardly to be relied on in matters which involve thousands of pounds. But the human side has communicated no taint whatever to Holy Scripture. Every Word of God is pure and sure, whether viewed as the utterance of man or as the thought of God. Whatever of man there is in the enunciation of the message, there is nothing which can prevent its being implicitly received by us, since the man saith nothing on his own account, but covers his own personality with the sacred authority of, "Thus saith the Lord." C. H. Spurgeon

These sentiments are further amplified in a review of *The Bible Educator*: "What right have we to be prying into 'the way of the Spirit,' and defining how He acts with this mind or the other, when He is presenting us with Scripture which is all inspired and all intended for our learning? The question of the manner of inspiration... is a mere intrusion into realms beyond us, and always leads to misunderstandings. If a man believes the Holy Scriptures to be infallibly and divinely inspired we are quite content; if he then goes on to talk about differences of modus, etc., we are off to our work, having other fish to look after." (1873, 566)

Perhaps the most poignant and forceful writing about inspiration was when he set down some *Sweet Experiences* while at Menton for the last time. They were written to "bare his soul" for the sake of some of his closest friends. Thus he wrote:

One reason why some of us would fight tooth and nail for our Bibles, is the fact that we have **felt** their inspiration.

I abhor the superstition of those who would fish for texts in the Bible as though they would find direction according to the page which they happened to open; this is to make Holy Scripture the tool of witchery, and to treat the Word of the Lord as though it were a wizard's charm. We reverence the sacred volume far too much to make it a sort of spiritual lottery, or Book of Fate, after the manner of the semi-heathen superstitions which survive among the credulous. But, when a passage from the Book of God has been made to shine within the mind and reveal itself to the heart by the power of the Holy Ghost, it ceases to become a question as to whether it is to be obeyed or not, for it forces itself upon the soul, and impresses its divine teaching upon the entire man. To the believer who received the sacred Word in the fullness of a divine application, it is a voice from the excellent glory, which he delights to hear; and as he hears, he lives by a new supply of energy and under a fresh anointing of heavenly grace. (1892, 2)

With such a faith in the divine inspiration of the Scriptures, no wonder he was able to review *Biblical Difficulties, and How to Meet Them*, with these devastating words: "As far as part of this book is concerned, [a more accurate title] would have been *Biblical Difficulties, and How to Increase Them!*" (1892, 214)

He had no such difficulties and once said, "If two things in Scripture appear to contradict each other, I believe them both!" No wonder the Bible was at the foundation of all his preaching and teaching, the bed-rock for all his philanthropic endeavours. No wonder that the God of the Bible blessed all that this "man of the Book" said, wrote and did.

### Translation

Today some people would refer to Spurgeon as a fundamentalist because he believed in the verbal inspiration of the Bible. He was not, however, an obscurantist, believing that the Authorized or King James's Version of the Bible was "let down from heaven on a piece of string," and "since it was good enough for Paul, it's good enough for me!" He believed in modern translations of the Bible, or versions that endeavoured to get closer to the original documents. He studied such new translations, reviewed them in *The Sword and the Trowel* and occasionally preached from a text taken, say, from the Revised Version. More light is thrown on his attitude to different translations in his magazines than in his messages from the pulpit. He was, for instance, very praiseworthy of any translation that **translated**, and did not **transliterate**, the Greek word for "baptism." He could not stand that word being "dressed up in English letters" rather than its true meaning being given. Thus when reviewing the first part of *The New Testament: a New Translation* by J. B. Rotherham (to be completed in ten or twelve parts), he wrote:

> A scrupulous attention to the meaning of the original [has been given, and] great care has been taken to bring out the shades of meaning involved in the presence or absence of the Greek article, and the different tenses of the verbs employed. To our staunch Baptist friends, one extract from a foot note under the name of John the Immerser will suffice we think to induce them to subscribe at once and so make the venture of the translator a pecuniary success. (1868, 379)

He had the same commendation for *The New Testament translated from the Purest Greek* by John Bowes:

> The translator, at any rate, is honest and executes his work to the best of his judgment (Matt. 3:1 & 2--John the Immerser). We are glad to see the foreign word "baptist" put out, and a translation given; this we hope the present revisers of the Bible will have the honesty to do also, as we would rather see any translation than none at all; our wish being if a word means "sprinkler" to have it put so, but if not, either let them translate it fairly or confess inability for the work in hand. (1870, 542/3)

J. N. Darby's translation came in for severe criticism, calling it a "one man's Bible" and "tampering with the text." (1884, 39)

He believed some alterations to the "Authorized" were very necessary and thought the Revised English Bible as a good idea. He wrote of it:

> Here is our own English Bible with its mistranslations amended, and its obsolete words and coarse phrases removed, so that it can be read in families without the need to omit certain verses on account of the children... Not one word is altered more than it needed to be, nor are the thoughts recast, it is our own grandmother's Bible, with many a blunder of the translators set to rights. (1877, 438)

Three years later he was commending the *Anglo-American Bible Revision* as proposed in twenty short essays by an American revision committee. He agreed that there was a need "for a thorough revision of the English Bible," especially as it was to be "performed in a truly conservative spirit." Would it at once supersede the "old and familiar book which has been in use for nearly three centuries? We devoutly hope it will be found worthy to do so. There are divisions enough among Protestants without encountering the danger of two different Bibles in the public sanctuary and in the private household. From such perils God forfend us. (1880, 130)

Not only did he welcome many new translations but pamphlets and books that pointed out the need for such new editions. He thought *Many Versions, but One Bible*, a paper on the Revised New Testament, an "admirable dissertation." Spurgeon had come to see that the Revised Version was "not accepted by the church at large as the successor of the Authorized Version, nor will it ever be. It is a good version, and in some respects, the best yet produced, but it must be made far better before it can be compared in all respects with the Bible of our youth, and it will even then be long before it supplants it. (1882, 144)

*The Revisers' English*, a book criticizing the English of the Revised Version, was not commended by Spurgeon. The author's manner was too "severe and caustic." He did not like the way "he seems to see evil, and only evil, in the Revised Version... There are many arguments in favour of the older Version as against the

Revised, and especially upon the point of its English; but [the author] spoils his case with extravagance of blame. We love the dear old Book in its old inimitable beauty, but we do not care for this narrow and scathing championship." Then Spurgeon himself becomes "severe and caustic" in his review's sting in the tail: "The best part of the volume is the group of photographs of the revisers!" (Ibid, 440)

By contrast he liked *Mistranslated Passages in our Bible: a Help for English Readers.* Spurgeon agreed with the author that "our Authorized version of the Old Testament is often sadly inaccurate. Little errors abound at which skeptics sneer, and pious people are strangely puzzled. The text and the translation both need to be carefully revised... The most determined courage and the most delicate caution must be called into play if it is to be done satisfactorily." (Ibid, 494)

*The Parallel Bible* Spurgeon described as "a magnificent copy of the sacred Word. Here we have the Authorized and Revised Versions in parallel columns, and the whole printed on the thinnest and finest of paper. What a present to a well-beloved pastor! We cannot suggest anything better, especially if bound in the best style. We are greatly obliged to Mr. Frowde for bringing out such a very useful edition of the Scriptures. (1890, 242)

On the other hand *The One Gospel; or, The Combination of the Narratives of the Four Evangelists in one Complete Record*, although compiled by fellow evangelical and friend, A. T. Pierson, was not so valuable as an aid to Bible study. His chief objection was that "as a compilation [it was] a human work and is liable to errors of arrangement; and furthermore, that it necessarily causes us to lose those lights and shades which are brought out in each of the gospels by the distinct object of its writer. (1891, 245)

Rare Bibles, ancient and antique versions, fascinated him. In his "Notes", he recorded a visit with a gentleman "who possessed a very large and valuable collection of Bibles, some of which are mainly remarkable because of the mistakes from which they derive their names. Two of these are the 'vinegar' Bible, and the 'wicked' Bible." This reminded him that "many people who would not read the Bible, would read them (i.e. Christians), and he hoped none of them would "be 'vinegar' through sour tempers or 'wicked' with inconsistent lives." (Ibid, 349)

Bible "competitions" he could not stand. He gave an example of a £20 prize being offered for "the number of times the word "Jesus" is contained in the gospels. If people were foolish or wicked enough to degrade the Word of God in this fashion, it might be their own concern rather than ours; but (he denied all knowledge) of the "great Mr. Spurgeon" [approving] of these competitions... Whoever "the great Mr. Spurgeon" may be, we cannot tell; but if Charles Haddon Spurgeon is meant, there is no truth in the statement; for "he does not approve of these competitions, and he has never said that 'they do much good, and are really profitable'. They may be profitable to those who get them up; but those who have sent in their little money have received nothing in return." (1890, 585)

Bible marking did not meet with his whole-hearted approval either. Reviewing *How To Mark Your Bible* by Mrs. Stephen Menzies he wrote:

> Whether Bibles marked with railway connections and other lines are of much after-value we cannot say from experience, but the process of marking must so engage the mind, and so beautifully call attention to parallels and consecutive ideas, that it must be quite a training for Bible readers. Anything which leads to **searching** the Scriptures is most useful... Oh, that we had more who are at home in every street and lane of Scripture! We should then have far fewer tolerating the snarling dogs who roam over the Bible as if it were a heap of dust from which they could root out a bone to growl over. Exposition is the best defense of Scripture. (1891, 532)

What he would have made of our plethora of reading-through-the-Bible-in-a-year systems and edited Bibles it is difficult to say. From a review of *Studies in the Life and Character of Peter*, we note that he was not in favor of "three chapters each weekday and five on Sundays" to get through the Bible in a year, with a few Psalms and Proverbs in each day, plus a brief extract from the New Testament. The book he was reviewing had an introductory chapter on Bible-reading. Spurgeon's review condemned the "reading of a chapter every day has a talismanic charm about it and may almost prove a passport to heaven. Even such a superstitious reading is better than none, for it may, perchance, put the reader in the way of a blessing; but how much better to study the Bible in a sensible, common sense manner, as we would any other book whose meaning we desired to reach. Always to take the Bible in small doses is not fair to the sacred volume; let it be read consecutively and the run of its teaching followed with devout care. No one would think of reading Milton, taking a stanza at a time... The Bible is so marvellous a book that even its fragments are precious as gold, but to know the divine teaching of the inspired Word it must be studied as a whole; for a whole it is." (1888, 140)

Pictorial Bibles are not a modern invention, such as today's Good News Bible. Reviewing *The Holy Bible, with Explanatory Notes, References, and a condensed Concordance*, he delighted in such "a marvellous book, crowded with illustrations and those of the best kind. It bears the palm as a Family Bible. The artistic talent displayed in the engravings must have cost the spirited publishers an immense sum, and we wonder how they can afford to sell the work at the price at which they offer it. There are notes to it, but the illustrations are the grand feature, and they are incomparable. This is the Bible which we select to give as a present to newly-married couples, and we would give every wedded pair a copy if our purse were but long enough." (1873, 475)

He was just as enamoured of *The Emphatic Diaglott*, which deserved "to hold a place in the first rank of the many valuable works that have issued from the American religious press. The idea is excellent, and the execution leaves little to be desired... The principal features which distinguish this from other modern versions of the New Testament are the *Interlinearly Word for Word English Translation*, and the *Signs of Emphasis*. Of the *Interlineary Translation* it would be difficult to speak too highly. It is well and carefully and faithfully executed, and is calculated to be very useful, not to those only who are unacquainted with Greek, but to all save the profoundest scholars, who are almost as familiar with the languages of the Bible as with their own mother tongue."

He not only desired its success personally but hoped that it would be "beside the desk of every divinity student and every preacher of the gospel." (Ibid, 565)

For Spurgeon, then, the Word of God was divinely-inspired, authoritative, practical and comprehensive. Like the Puritans he believed the sacred Book was sufficient for all faith and conduct. The Bible determined doctrine, worship, church order and government, and in private affected the Christian's life at home and away, at work and at play, his dress and his daily duty. The whole of life was to be seen by the light of God's Word, the believer's "lamp for his feet and light for his path." All this he wrote about in his "Notes", his book reviews and in special articles for *The Sword and the Trowel*. That this mine of information regarding C. H. Spurgeon and the Bible has been largely ignored perhaps explains why few, if any, major biographies of the Prince of Preachers include a separate chapter on Spurgeon and the Bible.

## CHAPTER TEN

# Calvinism and Arminianism

There are those of the Reformed School, belonging to churches with a marked Calvinistic emphasis, who tend to make Spurgeon rather a hyper-Calvinist. There are others who tend to look upon him as a more moderate follower of the great Geneva theologian. Then there are the conservative-evangelicals who would rather emphasize his love or Christian charity towards Arminian preachers and his support of evangelists such as D. L. Moody. Certainly Whitefield was his "hero" (some would say his model), yet it was the two Wesleys he lectured on and presented to the Christian public the published lecture. Perhaps extracts of an autobiographical nature culled from *The Sword and the Trowel* will help to correct misconceptions, bias and prejudice, and so give us a more correct conception of the Calvinistic/Arminianism beliefs dealt with by C. H. Spurgeon.

## Calvinism

Spurgeon was sometimes referred to as "the last of the Puritans;" he was also lampooned as "the last of the Calvinists." He himself, of course, stoutly denied this. Reviewing *Lectures on Preaching* by Henry Ward Beecher he suggested that they be read by young men "with the best filter within their reach... there are passages of the most mischievous kind which we greatly deplore." One such passage had to do with himself and his Calvinistic beliefs. He quotes the very words of Beecher "for (their) infelicity."

> Is it not true that Spurgeon is a follower of Calvin, and is he not an eminent example of success? In spite of it, yes; but I do not believe that the camel travels any better, or is any more useful as an animal, for the hump on its back.

For Beecher, Calvinism was to Spurgeon as the hump was to

the camel. Spurgeon pointed out that the hump was not a mistake, for the camel's Maker had so designed it. Naturalists agreed that the hump served a very useful purpose, the Arabs judging the condition of the camel by the size of its hump. The camel also feeds upon its hump as it crosses deserts. It is not again fit for a long journey until its hump has filled out again. For Spurgeon, "Calvinism is the spiritual meat which enables a man to labour on in the ways of Christian services; and, though ridiculed as a hump by those who are only lookers on, those who traverse the weary paths of a wilderness experience, know too well its value to be willing to part with it, even if a Beecher's splendid talents could be given in exchange." (1872, 479)

In reviewing *The Evangelical Revival and other Sermons* by R. W. Dale he strongly criticized the author for suggesting *"Mr. Spurgeon stands alone among the modern leaders of Evangelical Nonconformists in his fidelity to the older Calvinistic creed."* Spurgeon's reply to such an unjust insinuation was: *"If it be so we are sorry to hear it, and we pray God that it may not long be true"* (1881, 85). Perhaps this is why he always emphasized the teaching in his Pastor's College was "Calvinistic," although he did admit students who were Arminian by belief and practice.

Over six years before Dale's pronouncement Spurgeon had pronounced Calvinism was in good heart. He was then reviewing *The Other Side of Things* and was astonished to read the author say that "John Wesley gave Calvinism its death-blow." Spurgeon replied, "He might as reasonably have said that Cardinal Wiseman gave Protestantism its death-blow. Calvinism was never in better heart than now, and its power over human minds will increase as time rolls on, for although it does not comprehend all truth, it takes so clear a view of the Godward side of it, that it must abide." (1875, 42)

In *The Life of John Calvin*, which was "Calvin drawn by a strong Calvinist," again Spurgeon had to stress when reviewing the book that "We do not believe that Calvinism is dead, but on the contrary we believe that its essential spirit permeates all Evangelical Christendom. Wherein it is out of fashion for a while, it matters not; for, as the wheel of public opinion revolves, it will probably be again in the ascendant within another twenty years... it can never be crushed out while Holy Scripture remains." (1885, 141)

He even saw Calvinism alive and well in the Church of England. When reviewing *Substitution*, the author an Anglican rector, he said:

We bless God that there is yet "a remnant according to the election of Grace" left in the Church of England. This six-penny pamphlet inculcates particular redemption (i.e. one of the *Five Points of Calvinism*) in that downright, hearty, honest style which becomes daily more and more rare. (1874, 487)

Spurgeon himself, however, was never "tied down to the five points," nor did he try to influence others to be so restricted. In an address at the commencement of a college session he spoke thus:

I have never concealed the fact that the views we hold are pre-eminently evangelical, and of the form which is commonly called Calvinistic--not in any close or narrow sense, but in the sense of giving prominence to the grace of God. We have not attempted to tie men down to think exactly alike upon the five points, or fifty points, of matters wherein there is fair room for difference without sacrificing foundation truths; but we have always held by the infallible inspiration of the Bible, and we have also held that the essence of the revelation made to us in Holy Scripture is salvation by grace through faith in the precious blood of Jesus. Exceeding dear to us are the doctrines which we hold in common with all Protestant Christians, and also those which come more distinctly under the head of "the doctrines of grace." (1888, 569)

No wonder he was glad to read in *Soul-winning; or, Church Life and Growth* that the author, a Methodist, had written a "dainty morsel" which he could not forbear quoting. Before doing so he gave a few words of telling autobiography:

When so many are abusing him, it is sweet to see that, long ago, the minister of the Tabernacle was a co-worker with others in influencing earnest lives in regions beyond the Baptist community; yes, and beyond that "narrow

Calvinism" which is supposed to be his grievous weakness. There are thousands who have never complained of that supposed narrowness, but have been content to take the Lord's own gospel, even from the hand of one who has never concealed his delight in the doctrines of grace."

The "dainty-morsel" in the author's Preface contained these heart-warming words for Charles Haddon Spurgeon: "At the time of my candidature for the ministry, *I was favoured by hearing Charles Haddon Spurgeon preach* . . . and who has not heard the great preacher of the Tabernacle?" (1888, 87)

Not only were the Calvinistic doctrines dear to Spurgeon, even his "name... is as music to our ears." He called him "that peerless man." No wonder he reviewed *Young Calvin in Paris* with great sympathy. He ended his review with this brief heart-felt prayer: "O that the God of Calvin were more manifestly with us in this land." (1868, 91-92)

For Spurgeon, heaven would be the final place of proof that the doctrines of Calvin were the right ones. Reviewing *The Living Sacrifice*, a Primitive Methodist book, he was first of all amused to read the words: "Went to Stroud to hear the Rev. Charles Haddon Spurgeon. A rank Calvin, but I believe a good man!" Spurgeon concluded his review by saying that "among the glorified this warm-hearted herald of the cross now rests from his labours, and has become a 'rank Calvin' himself, for the doctrines of grace are the theology of the blood-washed before the throne." (1870, 283)

### Arminianism

Staunch Calvinist that he was, Spurgeon never denounced those of opposing views or withdrew his fellowship from them. Rather he tried to see how much Calvinism there was in their Arminianism, of what common ground in the gospel they shared so that they could have fellowship together. When reviewing *A Homiletic Analysis of the New Testament* by Dr. Joseph Parker he emphasized their differences: "We are certainly as wide as the poles asunder on the matter of election;" and he said that "we are opposed to the school of theology to which the writer belongs," but then ended on this gracious note: "The book... is a serviceable one, and contains many striking suggestions which will start trains of thought and thus help many readers to new and fuller views of some truths which are eminently worthy of their regard." (1870, 236)

*The Student's Handbook of Christian Theology* was a handbook "of Wesleyan divinity," yet he "rated it very highly, being scholarly, well-arranged and carefully executed." It contained "attacks upon the Calvinistic side of truth," yet he recommended it for the "truths which are common to all Christians." Of its Arminian views he merely remarked that "brethren of Arminian views will find this book a most admirable compendium of their opinions." (Ibid, 137)

What greater commendation could an Arminian have than:

"We wish all our Calvinistic friends were even a tenth part as useful as Father Taylor of California, the apostle of South Africa. We have given extracts from the work... in other parts of the Magazine." Yet this author's theology was "ultra-Arminian." In spite of that Spurgeon wrote that "there is a savour of the living power of God about his spirit." (1867, 285)

This was also Spurgeon's attitude towards the American evangelist D. L. Moody. To most people's mind Moody was the outstanding Arminian of Spurgeon's day, yet Charles Haddon Spurgeon spoke highly of him, recommended him to the readers of his magazine, sent his Pastor's College students to his meetings and engaged him as a pulpit supply at the Tabernacle while he was at Menton. We can hardly see pastors of the Reformed School today taking such an attitude to, say, Dr. Billy Graham.

In spite of Sankey playing "a bag of whistles" or an American organ, Spurgeon referred to Moody and Sankey as "those two consecrated evangelists" and published a lengthy article about them in *The Sword and the Trowel*. (1875, 115)

He regretted that a critical pamphlet had been published by Dr. Kennedy when Spurgeon judged D. L. Moody "to be *sent by God* to bless our land in an unusual degree." Fortunately he had faith to believe that "the work which God is doing is so great and manifest that it cannot be injured by any man's comment upon it." (Ibid, 142)

When D. L. Moody first preached at the Tabernacle, Spurgeon warned his readers that "there is sure to be a dense crowd," and "the place will be full." But he added: "We hope that on some future occasion both Mr. Moody and Mr. Sankey will conduct a series of services at the Tabernacle." (1881, 583)

Spurgeon himself took part in two of Moody's meetings in Croydon and also sent his students to the services when he was "more and more impressed with a sense of the remarkable power which rests upon the beloved Moody." (1884, 294)

Moody's Sunday at the Tabernacle while Spurgeon was at Menton was well-reported in the magazine, Spurgeon declaring: "Their hold upon the multitude has by no means diminished." (1882, 42)

His own evangelists, Messrs. Fullerton and Smith, were frequently criticized, even in a Baptist newspaper. Some thought the were too Calvinistic whereas Spurgeon said, "We might have found fault with [the] zealous brethren for their Arminianism; but we have not done so, because we regarded it as a frequent infirmity of noble minds!"

Such "noble minds" as Dr. Barnardo and General Booth, both of Arminian persuasion, Spurgeon admired and supported in their philanthropic and other endeavours: "Dr. Barnardo is one of the greatest of them and [so are] his many noble enterprises." (1875, 44) "We do not agree with certain of the doctrines here taught" such as Mrs. Booth's *Popular Christianity*; and although "we do not pronounce any opinion upon the Salvation Army methods," he was in agreement with their stand against "dangerous evils" and their "faith in the gospel." With his intense dislike for militarism he objected to Booth's army-style uniform and ranks, but he liked their love for souls and their desire to go for the worst, even if their preaching were Arminian.

Another contemporary Arminian of "noble mind" was Dr. Joseph Parker. As we have already seen, Spurgeon always criticized his Arminianism when reviewing his books, but that did not prevent their fellowship in the gospel or a proposed exchange of pulpits. In his magazine, Spurgeon thanked Parker for his "most generous impulse" which led him "on a sudden to make a collection for the Orphanage." He thanked Parker for his "warm brotherly letter," and although it was not meant for the press, proceeded to print it in full in *The Sword and the Trowel*. So Arminian doctrine in the Tabernacle from Moody, and Arminian money for the Orphanage from Parker--surely there is a lesson here for today. Did big heartedness end with the Victorian era? As long as the essentials of the gospel are believed-in and preachers are trying to win the lost, surely there is no case for "sniping" at one another. We should rejoice, as Spurgeon did, that there are points on which both Calvinists and Arminians can agree.

Reviewing *The Life of Jabez Bunting*, Spurgeon said of him,

> Dr. Bunting was an Evangelical Arminian... he was one of those Arminians who would never have been distinguished from Calvinists had not Calvinists themselves in some cases gone beyond the line of truth. He sucked the honey though he left the comb. Dr. Bunting himself we find clear as a bell on the doctrine of justification by faith. Certain passages from the close of his biography will show the reader how in his inmost soul he believed in sovereign grace. (1888, 191)

So convinced was Spurgeon that Calvinists and Arminians had much they could agree on that in his magazine he reprinted a short article from the American *Hamilton Review*. He entitled it, "Wherein Arminian and Calvinist agree." It was an imaginary conversation between Mr. Wesley and Mr. Simeon and deserves to be reprinted here in full:

> Pray, sir, do you feel yourself a depraved creature, so depraved that you would never have thought of turning to God, if God had not first put it into your heart?" "Yes," said the veteran Wesley, "I do, indeed." And do you utterly despair of recommending yourself to God by anything that you can do, and look for salvation solely through the blood and righteousness of Christ?" "Yes, solely through Christ." "But, sir, supposing you were first saved by Christ, are you not, somehow or other, to save yourself afterwards by your own works?" "No, I must be saved by Christ from

first to last." "Allowing, then, that you were first turned by the grace of God, are you not, in some way or other, to keep yourself by your own power?" "No." "What, then, are you to be upheld every hour and every moment by God, as much as an infant in its mother's arms?" "Yes, altogether." "And is all your hope in the grace and mercy of God to preserve you unto his heavenly kingdom?" "Yes, I have no hope but in him." "Then, sire, with your leave, I will put up my dagger again; for this is all my Calvinism; this is my election, my justification by faith; my final perseverance; it is, in substance, all that I hold, and as I hold it." (1886, 491)

**CHAPTER ELEVEN**

# Evangelists and Enquirers

*Stand Up and Be Counted* is the title of a book by Dr. R. T. Kendall. In it he defends the practice of what is known as "the altar call" in America. In this country it is well-known through the visits of Dr. Billy Graham for his crusades in which he invites enquirers to "Get up out of your seat" and come to the front of the auditorium.

Many evangelists use the same procedure, with variations, at their smaller missions or campaigns. Besides asking those to whom God has been speaking in the message to "come to the front," others ask for "heads down and hands up;" that is, Christian are to bow in prayer while enquirers raise their hands to be prayed for by the evangelist. If the meeting-place is small or crowded, another method is to ask enquirers to stand up from their seat while they are prayed for.

Those of the Reformed School are, in general, opposed to such invitations and try to make out a good case for Spurgeon being against them as well. While he may not have invited enquirers to come to the front of his Tabernacle (by the very nature of the architecture of the building that would have been impossible with a crowd of over 6,000 in the congregation), there are indications that he used some form of dealing with enquirers at the end of a service when he was preaching elsewhere. He certainly did not refrain from supporting others (e.g. D. L. Moody) who practiced it, nor did he stay away from meetings where he knew the practice would be carried out.

The volumes of *The Sword and the Trowel* provide little-known and little-used insights into Spurgeon's real attitude to evangelistic methods of helping enquirers to "stand up and be counted."

## Evangelists

Space prevents much being reproduced from Spurgeon's magazine about evangelists. He not only appointed his own evangelists such as W. Y. Fullerton and Manton Smith, but he also founded an Evangelists' Association which is given little mention in many of the biographies of Spurgeon. The College also had its own Society of Evangelists which supported three evangelists, but the Evangelists' Association had "a different sphere of labour" which was carried out because of their belief that "the Lord has qualified certain men who would be attached to churches in the Metropolis. (1878, 587ff) They also held open-air meetings on the Tabernacle steps and went into schools wherever possible.

The evangelists of the College's Society of Evangelists, by contrast, were not limited by the boundaries of the Metropolis. They had *carte blanche* to accept invitations through the British Isles. When one of the first to be appointed, A. J. Clarke, had to emigrate to Australia for his health's sake, his place was taken by W. Y. Fullerton. He and J. Manton Smith formed a "happy partnership for the Lord" and travelled together throughout the United Kingdom. Each month in Spurgeon's "Notes" he gave up-to-date news of their missions, and they are far too numerous to be reproduced.

There is one important "Note" in 1880 that tells us something of the kind of men Spurgeon chose to be his evangelists and the kind of preaching they engaged in. They were "all-rounders," taking not only main evangelistic meetings but Bible readings, children's meetings, Band of Hope meetings and tea meetings for those "brought to a knowledge of the truth through the instrumentality of the evangelists."

As to their preaching, "their theology is that of the old Puritans. They preach ruin by the fall; redemption, regeneration, and justification by faith, in the old style and with the old results;" (this rather conflicts with the Arminian/Calvinistic characteristics given in our previous chapter). Fullerton was "young--a circumstance which his critics cannot forget, and which his friends thankfully remember." His preaching, in particular, was "simply wonderful" when expressing the primary truths of

Christianity, and he had "a power of adapting himself to the varying needs of each audience." (1880, 43, 44)

Manton Smith, on the other hand, played a more supporting role and led the singing, using his silver trumpet to great effect; at one mission it was reported "there was the usual amount of gospel singing and graphic stories... till eight o'clock, by which time the congregation had grown large." This rather smacks of today's American "warm-up" methods, condemned by those of the Reformed School. But there is more. "Some few held up their hands in token that they desired the prayers of God's people, and others stayed behind to be spoken to by the workers who were watching for souls." (1890, 43) And there were "special services at the Tabernacle" with Spurgeon present. Previously, on the Sunday evening, "Mr. Fullerton divided with Charles Haddon Spurgeon the time usually allotted to a sermon, and preached on his portion... admirably." (Ibid)

On the Thursday night a special, extra meeting was held by popular vote and there was a "flock of enquirers." While the following week, at the Sunday evening service, "scores rose in different parts of the building, declaring their desire to be Christ's" and in a meeting for enquirers afterwards in the lower Lecture Hall, "it was touching... to watch many scores of people rising, one after another, and, in response to the question, whether they would be Christ's saying, 'I will;' 'I will.'" (Ibid, 44)

### Enquirers

The above example of the way Spurgeon's evangelists dealt with enquirers is not given to suggest that this was also his way. He certainly allowed it and was happy to be present during it, but the final paragraph to the above description of blessing at the Tabernacle during a fortnight's special services contains these words:

> We have noticed that our converts at the Tabernacle are very few of them of a hasty sort... Enquiry rooms are not much used by us, for the people go home to their gracious friends and are helped in the heavenward way by those

who know them best; or else they come again to hear the gospel, and the Lord meets with them, and removes their difficulties." But then he graciously added: "That which is admirable with one congregation may not suit another." (Ibid, 45)

Perhaps that is why he gave prominence to a paper that had been read at a meeting of ministers by reprinting it in his magazine. The author, a former student of the Pastor's College, gave these guidelines: "Invite seekers to remain for conversation in the vestry... request the anxious to remain in their seats while the rest leave... an inquirer should be dealt with on the spot, whilst his sense of sin is vivid and fresh." (1865, 45 & 46)

After a series of special prayer meetings, at the end of which Spurgeon pleaded "with God for anxious and careless souls present," then "many anxious ones [retired into a room below], several of whom received peace with God through faith in the precious Saviour. Many of these have since been seen by Mr. Spurgeon." (Ibid, 70)

During the same special week, "Charles Haddon Spurgeon earnestly exhorted those who had accepted Christ as their Saviour to come forward amongst his people and avow their attachment to His person and name." (Ibid) That meeting was held on a Wednesday evening at Providence Chapel, Shoreditch, so obviously Spurgeon felt he could do something different on a week-night and not in his own Tabernacle.

Another night, in Abbey Road Chapel, St. John's Wood, after an address by Spurgeon, Pastor Scott gave an appeal, and there was "an instant response... by a number of persons... he implored exercised souls to take God at His Word, and at once to receive Christ as their only Saviour. There were those in the assembly who felt constrained to follow this counsel." (Ibid, 71)

A month later another outreach prayer meeting was held at the Tabernacle with a congregation between 6,000 and 7,000. Several short addresses were given, interspersed with prayer. The last message was given by Spurgeon himself, and then he "closed with prayer. Inquirers were then encouraged to retire to the Lecture Hall, where ministers and elders would be glad to converse with them; and many responded to the invitation." (Ibid, 128)

The present writer's late grandfather was by now "sitting under Spurgeon," having moved, like Spurgeon, from Essex to London. He frequently described for his grandson the thrill of seeing elders and other personal workers, waiting at the ends of the pews for any anxious enquirers. This was essential on those Sundays when the regular congregation was asked to stay away so that others might take their place.

This happened on August 19, 1877, and Spurgeon described the scene in his own words in his "Notes":

> The house was soon packed in every corner by a congregation in which the male element very far predominated. The audience was singularly mixed, a large number being persons from the West End, while others were evidently new to places of worship. In the judgment of our most reliable brethren, it was the best service we ever had; to God be the glory. Some two or three hundred remained, professedly in an anxious state, and many more were conversed with by workers, who were dotted here and there all over the place. Several confessed Christ, and rejoiced in His salvation, and we hope fruit will appear in days to come, as well as on the spot. (1877, 442)

It is difficult to see the difference between on the spot conversions through an open appeal to "come to the front," and those being directed to a separate room or to nearby personal workers, especially as the architecture of the Tabernacle did not lend itself to several hundred standing at the front. Yet, from time to time Spurgeon stated: "Those converted under our ministry are seldom of the "after-meeting" kind--excited and over-persuaded. They usually go their way and think the matter over and come forward to confess their faith when they have tried themselves and tested their conversion; hence we believe that we have as yet seen only the advance-guard of the army of converts." (1883, 562)

He amplified this in a book review the following year. It was called *The Enquiry-room: Hints for Dealing with the Anxious*.

Although urging young workers to purchase the book "and profit by its wise suggestions" his personal view was: "As to the Enquiry-room itself, we have little confidence in it as a standing institution, or in its results where much is made of it. We might grieve many if we were to say what we know the dreadful disappointment experienced by those who look up Enquiry-room converts. An immediate interview seems to be an admirable plan for reaching the heart, and so it may be if used occasionally; but the tendency is to force on an imaginary decision, or produce a hasty faith in the room instead of a quiet faith in Jesus." (1884, 555)

So why did his Tabernacle Lecture Hall become an enquiry room so frequently? Was it because he knew his elders were well able to control excessive emotion and interview in a sane and sensible way, or was it because he knew that eventually he would be interviewing the same converts personally when they came to him requesting baptism and church membership?

As we have seen, his own evangelists used this method, and he was always glad to include this sort of report of their activities in his monthly "Notes":

> The last meeting was remarkable beyond any, and the enquiry-room was too small for all the anxious souls to be dealt with in it. (1887, 43)

He even included a report of Fullerton and Smith which described not only how many came into the enquiry-room nightly, but "on Monday evening above fifty stood up to acknowledge having received Christ during the meeting, and another fifty to confess anxiety about their souls." (1888, 200)

In 1891, the year before he died, Spurgeon was getting weaker and needed help with the services. He enlisted the aid of the Rev. W. Stott of St. John's Wood and "frequently an after-meeting might follow a service, and an earnest brother like Mr. Scott would conduct it when we could not." (1891, 93)

Obviously Mr. Stott would not arrange an after-meeting without Spurgeon's permission and approval, and it sounds as if Spurgeon would have conducted it if he had had the physical strength. Eternity alone will reveal which method of dealing with anxious souls Spurgeon favoured most and whether the converts stood fast after being counselled in after-meeting and enquiry-room or personally by Spurgeon after they had returned home and God had dealt with them in the privacy of their own room. All we can surmise from Spurgeon's "Notes" and book reviews is that like the Apostle Paul he was prepared "by all means to save some."

CHAPTER TWELVE

# Prayer-books and Prayer-mats

It is a well known fact and an often repeated quotation that Spurgeon gave the secret of his success to some visitors to the Tabernacle as, "My people pray for me." The year before he died he wrote in his magazine "Notes":

> If we value any one form of meeting above another, next to the Breaking of Bread, we esteem the Meeting for Prayer and Praise. So long as the prayer-meetings are sustained, nothing will go greatly amiss; but if we slacken in the matter of united intercession, nothing can long be really right. (1891, 94)

**Tabernacle Prayer Meetings**

The weekly meeting of the church for prayer was held on Monday evenings at the Metropolitan Tabernacle. Reporting on one held on November 6, 1871, Spurgeon wrote in his "Notes":

> There were from ten to twelve hundred... we sent a trustworthy friend to see how many responded to the tinkling bell of our parish church, and counting priests and officials, male and female, there were only twenty-two persons present. (1871, 570)

The only reason Spurgeon crowed over such a crowd at the Tabernacle was because the Rector of Newington had told the Anglican Church Congress that he had influenced several young men into the Anglican ministry and "had done it under the eaves of Mr. Spurgeon's Tabernacle."

Several years later he wrote in his Notes:

> If anyone could drop in, and see the host which gathers to what is stigmatized by the modern men as "only a prayer meeting," or "a mere religious expedient," they would begin

to see what power gatherings for prayer may be made to possess. (1888, 563)

The church fellowship prayer meetings were not always held in the Tabernacle. Cottage prayer meetings were sometimes held. On one occasion

> some sixty meetings were thus commenced at the same hour, and from the letters received there appears to have been a general manifestation of the spirit of prayer in these household gatherings. The advantages are many in thus collecting small companies in private houses: friends are encouraged to pray before others who would never have done so in large assemblies, and the ice once being broken, they are prepared to take their turn in public another time... and the young people of the families where the prayer meetings are held are led to take an interest in the proceedings of the church... We print a list of houses open, send a student to each, and under the direction of the elders the whole business is a glad and joyful one. (1876, 141)

## Private and Public Prayer

In an inaugural address given to the conference of the Pastors' College, Spurgeon emphasized, among other subjects, the importance of private prayer in the spirit of Scripture--praying always. He said,

> We cannot be always on the knees of the body, but the soul should never leave the posture of devotion. The habit of prayer is good, but the spirit of prayer is better. Regular retirement is to be maintained, but continued communion with God is to be our aim. As a rule, we ministers ought never to be many minutes without actually lifting up our hearts in prayer. Some of us could honestly say that we are seldom a quarter of an hour without speaking to God and that not as a duty but as an instinct, a habit of the new nature for which we claim no more credit than a babe does for crying after its mother. (1876, 250)

He went on to give an even more graphic autobiographical detail of his practice of prayer:

To me my greatest secrecy in prayer has often been in public; my truest loneliness with God has occurred to me while pleading in the midst of thousands. I have opened my eyes at the close of a prayer and come back to the assembly with a sort of shock at finding myself on earth and among men. Such seasons are not at our command, neither can we raise ourselves into such a condition by any preparations or efforts. How blessed they are both to the minister and his people no tongue can tell! (Ibid)

No wonder there were many who declared that they were as much (if not more) affected by Spurgeon's public prayers than by his preaching. Even a reading of some of his prayers now in cold print gives us some idea of his inner solitude with God before the Throne of Grace while he prayed with his vast Tabernacle congregation. Mechanically it was a question of practice and more practice.

In a tailpiece entitled "Pray without ceasing" he wrote:

A celebrated performer upon the piano was continually familiar with his instrument, for he used to say, "If I quit the piano one day I notice it; if I quit two days **my friends** notice it; if I quit it three days **the public** notice it." No doubt he correctly described his experience; only by perpetual practice could he preserve the ease and delicacy of his touch. Be sure that it is so with prayer. If this holy art be neglected, even for a little time, the personal loss will be great; if the negligence be continued, our nearest spiritual friends will notice a deterioration in tone and life; and if the evil should be long indulged, our character and influence will suffer with a wider circle. To be a master of the mystery of prayer one must pray, pray continually, pray hourly, pray at all times, pray without ceasing. A Christian should no more leave off praying than the musician should leave off playing; in fact, it is the breath of every spiritual man, and woe be to him should he restrain it!" (1885, 484)

### Printed Prayers

Spurgeon had an intense dislike for written or printed prayers. He rarely has anything good to say about any book he reviews that deals with the subject of printed prayers. This one is typical:

> Our venerable friend (author of *Prayers in Retirement*) should certainly have a recommendatory word from us if we dared to give it, but we do so thoroughly dislike forms of prayer that even when he writes them we cannot say more than they are good for the sort; but the whole mess of written prayers is an abomination to us. A man can no more put true prayer into a book than he can put an angel into a cannon-ball. (1866, 238)

In one issue of the magazine he reviewed two books of written prayers together--both were for family use. "We recommend neither," he began, then went on:

> It is said in reference to family prayer that it is better to go on crutches than not at all, but our own belief is that the crutches create the lameness which they are supposed to remedy. We have no more sympathy with forms of prayer in households any more than in congregations. If timid believers strongly felt it to be their duty to pray in their families, they would ere long gird themselves to do so, and the Lord would graciously assist them; but as it is, these prayer-books come in as an arm of flesh upon which they can lean instead of crying to the strong for strength. (1870, 187)

Prayers for the aged and prayers for Sunday school teachers both received the same treatment. The former were contained in a book with large print for the aged to see well. But Spurgeon asked, "But should they be? We say, No... We dare not recommend any persons to use forms of prayer. If they are unbelievers, the forms will be a mockery and if believers, they will be a hindrance to the free Spirit." (1872, 432) The review of prayers for teachers began with "No, no, no! A thousand times No! We do not want forms of prayer for our Sunday schools. People who cannot pray cannot teach. When our teachers have to read prayers, the schools may as well be closed, for the power to bless and save the children will have clean departed. We will, for once, compose a prayer for a litany: "From all ready-made prayers in Sunday schools, deliver us." (1890, 40)

Spurgeon, of course, published his own book of family worship, *The Interpreter*, but it contained no "ready-made prayers" and so "the sale has been limited." (1878, 43) As he said when reviewing *Morning Family Prayers for a Year*: "Written prayers are like those dried plants which botanists show us in sheets of brown paper; the beauty and the perfume are gone, for there is no life in the *hortus siccus*." (1887, 85)

Changing the metaphor when reviewing *Prayers for Christian Families*, he said: "We go dead against ready-made prayers. They are like ready-made clothes; they are made to fit everybody and fit nobody!" (1890, 40)

To give added support to his abhorrence of written prayers he quotes John Bunyan in a review of *Prayers for a Month*. Having said that "the best forms of prayer are only clean shrouds for dead souls" and that "three words of living prayer are worth a ton weight of paper-prayer," he continues, "Here we may fitly introduce John Bunyan's estimate of written prayers in general and of the Prayer Book in particular, for we heartily unite in his testimony. 'The Apostles, when they were at the best, yea, when the Holy Ghost assisted them, yet then they were fain to come off with sighs and groans, falling short of expressing their mind, but with sighs and groans which cannot be uttered. But here, now, the wise men of our days are so well skilled, as that they have both the manner and matter of their prayers at their fingers' ends, setting such a prayer for such a day, and that twenty years before it comes. One for Christmas, another for Easter and six days after that. They have also counted how many syllables must be said in every one of them. For each Saint's Day also, they have them ready for the generations yet unborn to say. They can tell you also, when to kneel, when you shall stand, when you should abide in your seats, when you should go up into the chancel and what you should do when you come there. All which the Apostles came short of as not being able to compose so profound a matter. And that for this reason included in the Scripture, because the fear of God tied them to pray as they ought.'" (1871, 575)

Contemplation

By contrast with written prayers, or even spoken prayers, Spurgeon knew the value of silent prayer or contemplation. "Some of us," he wrote in his magazine (reprint of a Menton communion address) "speak oftener with Christ then we do with wife or child, and our communion with Jesus is deeper and more thorough than our fellowship with our nearest friend." He was referring to his habit of silent meditation or contemplation in the presence of the Living Lord:

> I like sometimes in prayer, when I do not feel that I can say anything, just to sit still and look up; then faith spiritually describes the Well-beloved and hears his voice in the solemn silence of the mind. Thus we have [conversation] with Jesus of a closer sort then any words could possibly express. Our soul melts beneath the warmth of Jesus' love and darts upward her own love in return. Think not that I am dreaming or am carried off by the memory of some unusual rhapsody: no, I assert that the devout soul can converse with the Lord Jesus all the day and can have as true fellowship with Him as if He still dwelt bodily among men. This thing comes to me, not by the hearing of the ear, but by my own personal experience: I know of a surety that Jesus manifests himself unto His people as He doth not unto the world. (1883, 54)

Spurgeon was not in any way a mystic experiencing communion with God without the intermediate stages of thought or speech. He had no time for visions or a state of ecstasy that brought about oneness with deity. The practical nature of his public prayers and his pragmatism expressed in sermons and philanthropic works give the lie to charges of mysticism. He was no nonconformist Thomas á Kempis or St. John of the Cross. He was "down to earth" in every sense, yet occasionally he found, like all Christians, "he knew not what to pray for as he ought" and then discovered

Prayer is the burden of a sigh,
The falling of a tear,

The upward glancing of an eye
When none but God is near.
James Montgomery

**Prayer Duration**

The story is apocryphal that Spurgeon once said in a prayer meeting, "While our brother is finishing his prayer we will sing hymn number so-and-so." D. L. Moody was the originator of that choice saying. Spurgeon would have approved of Moody's interruption, however, for he detested long prayers. He described them in these graphic words:

Personally, we have heard utterances in prayer meetings which were painfully like a continual tooth-drawing. They were hard, cold, heartless, dreary and both as long and as dismal as a winter's night. All of a sudden we thought and hoped that the brother had done; but, alas, he took up a fresh lease, and entered upon another lengthened period. To all appearance he was coming to a conclusion a second time, when off he went, like a shot which ricochets or a boy's stone which when thrown into the water goes duck – duck – drake upon the surface. The prayer was diluted to the dregs of nothing, but end there seemed to be none. Oh that the tooth were out! The beloved brother had said all that could be said and prayed for all that could be prayed for; but he evidently felt it necessary to begin again. We can have too much of a good thing in such a case, and we wish the friend thought so.

...Worst of all, however, and fullest development of Sir Fowell's simile, is the click, clack, click, clack, of a fluent female who has gained your ear and means to hold it.

...We have felt ready to open our mouth, and let her draw all of our teeth *seriatim*, if she would but leave off talking. She had nothing to say, and she said that nothing at extreme length with marvelous energy and with unwearied repetition. We have turned our head; we have shut our eyes; we have wished we had gun-cotton in our ears and dynamite in our brain, but our wishes did not deliver us; we were given over to the tormentor and must abide the fulfillment of our sentence... a continual tooth-drawing. (1880, 260)

Describing a personal incident in a prayer-meeting address entitled "Why we have not," he said:

I know a church which is endowed with an excellent deacon, a real Godly man, but he will pray without ceasing at every meeting, and I fear he will pray the prayer-meeting down to nothing unless he is soon taken home. The other night when he had talked for full twenty minutes he intimated both to heaven and earth that all he had said was merely a preface, a drawing near as he called it, and that he was then going to begin.

None of his friends were pleased to receive that information, for they had begun to cherish the hope that he would soon have done. They were all too sadly aware that now he would pray for our own beloved country, from the queen upon the throne to the peasant in the cottage, then for Australia and all the colonies, and then for China and India, starting off afresh with kindly expressions for the young and for the old, the sick, for sailors and for the Jews. As a rule, *nothing* was really asked for by this most estimable brother, but he uttered several pious remarks on all these subjects, and many more.

It is a great pity when highly esteemed brethren fall into the notion that they must deliver themselves of long harangues: the better the men the worse the evil, for then we are forced to tolerate them. I am sorry when a good man gets the idea that praying means telling out his experience or giving his theological opinions. I am told that our Salvation Army friends strike up a tune whenever a friend becomes long and prosy, and I have a great sympathy with the practice. It removes the responsibility of stopping the man from the minister to the people and by dividing the action among many it operates like a round robin for the screening of any one. (1881, 494)

No wonder Spurgeon gave a tailpiece entitled "Be short" on one page of his magazine. It was "a hint for the prayer-meeting" and carried some very useful advice for his readers, urging them to "try it... and let us know if you succeed. We will keep a register of such blessed calamities." The incident went as follows:

> A pastor is reported to have requested the brethren to omit the usual beginning and ending of their prayers. We have heard people ask to be forgiven for their shortcomings when we felt a deal more grieved for their longcomings. Half the pretty phrases in public devotion seldom go together. We never heard of any brother being blamed for being too short in prayer. We should like to hear of a prayer-meeting failing through the brevity of the petitions. (Ibid, 393)

All was not doom and gloom, however, whenever Spurgeon wrote about prayer, pointing out the pitfalls of people and the drawbacks of books of prayer. In his "Notes" he was often far from discouraging by giving remarkable answers to prayer.

**Answered Prayer**

One such incident concerned the wife of one of his college students:

> The first time I came up to London after I was married and brought my little baby with me to the Tabernacle, he disturbed the service by crying, but you prayed "for the little one whose voice we heard just now." You did not know who the little one was, but I stayed to shake hands with you, and you said, "Was that the little one that cried?" I said, "Yes." You said, "Well he got the benefit of a prayer." That was twenty-one years ago, last February.

The mother then went on to describe "a fatal accident which happened last March (1890) to a man who was working with her son, and that afterwards her boy wrote to tell her that he had found that "None but Jesus can do helpless sinners good!" (1891, 96)

Spurgeon was sure, in the penultimate year of his life, that his life had been prolonged through the prayers of his own Tabernacle members and the readers of his magazine. From Menton he wrote this brief note to be included in the next issue of the magazine:

> Dear Brethren,
>
> The Lord's name be praised for first giving and then hearing the loving prayers of his people! Through these prayers my life is prolonged. I feel greatly humbled, and very grateful, at being the object of so great a love and so wonderful an outburst of prayer. I have not the strength to say more. Let the name of the Lord be glorified! Yours most heartily, C. H. Spurgeon. (Ibid, 539)

## The Prayer Mat

We do not normally associate prayer mats with evangelical Christianity. Usually we relegate them, with prayer wheels, beads, paper handkerchiefs and all the rest of such superstitious nonsense to the place fitted for such paraphernalia of cults and false religion. Spurgeon, however, was once presented with some curiosities from the Congo by a missionary on furlough. Besides a spear and shield and a horn and a spoon, there was a mat. As always he made use of such things as an illustration in a sermon or an article for his magazine. He said of the mat:

> What was that for? It was the work of Arabs, and they make these things to use when they kneel in prayer. You have all heard of prayer-mats. Every minister needs the prayer even if he does not need the mat. One of our constant watchwords is, "Let us pray." The mat that has been sent to me is of considerable size and has room for several persons upon it. Indeed I have need of a big prayer mat. This Tabernacle with its College, Orphanage, Colportage, and Evangelistic work, and many other departments of service, needs perpetual prayer. "Brethren pray for us." (1887 134).

Every believer in Christ Jesus needs a "prayer mat". We may not be in prominent positions like Spurgeon or other ministers of the gospel; we may not have to oversee so many Christian agencies nor have the responsibilities, the cure of souls, towards a vast congregation and membership, but we do have our daily witness and service that needs to be undergirded with prayer.

## CHAPTER THIRTEEN

# 𝔓rogrammes and 𝔇iagrams

There is a true story told of a young man sitting for the entrance exam of Spurgeon's College. Asked to define and explain the term "eschatology" he wrote a one-word answer--"bell-ringing!" Perhaps he was not far from the truth, for when Christ comes again surely there will be campanology or bell-ringing in heaven. Just as that student was near, yet so far, from an explanation of eschatology, so serious students of Spurgeon's eschatology have usually missed the mark. By some he is described as a post-millennialist, by others as a pre-millennialist and by a few as an a-millennialist, although the latter doctrinal position had not yet been worked out in Victorian times.

The deficiency in the assessment of Spurgeon's eschatological position is that only his sermons are researched in the main. There are one or two references to *The Sword and the Trowel* by some writers, but they have not done their work thoroughly. Besides a few articles printed in the Tabernacle magazine, the untapped source of the magazine volumes has been neglected once again, especially Spurgeon's reviews of books to do with prophecy, the second coming, commentaries on the Book of Daniel and The Revelation, plus other aspects of eschatolgy or the doctrine of the Last Things.

Although Spurgeon did preach about the Second Coming, he was, as always, preaching the gospel "for a verdict." His remarks in the magazine were of a more autobiographical and academic nature. They do not give us a systematic body of teaching regarding Spurgeon's dispensational beliefs or his position regarding any other school of second coming thought. They do, however, when placed all together, give us an overall picture of his views about the event, the millennium, the new heaven and earth, bodily resurrection, final judgment and so on.

He obviously had more important, more essential things to do than become a student of prophecy. He saw no reason to become *au fait* with a "programme of the ages," and even if he believed in charts and diagrams, he could hardly use them in a church building so vast as the Tabernacle before the days of large video screens.

Spurgeon wrote when reviewing *A Bird's Eye View of Unfulfilled Prophecy*, "We do not see that our prophetic brethren win more souls to Jesus than others: we heartily wish they did... some of them have given up the world as hopeless." (1875, 446)

The ones who try to pigeon-hole Spurgeon and make him fit a particular school of prophecy say that if he were a pre-millennialist, then he became one only just before he died when he signed what is known as "Spurgeon's Creed." The above review denies that theory, for the review was written in 1875, and in it he said that he agreed with the author, who was a pre-millennialist, but could not agree with him in saying that "disbelief in the pre-millennial advent brings great evils upon the church." (Ibid)

In another review he said that "we fear we are hopelessly incapable of profiting by modern prophetic writings," not, we notice, from studying prophecy but from a perusal of the writings and findings of others. (1869, 139)

His reason for finding prophetic books so unprofitable was that "there are few reasonable men to maintain and declare this truth, for never was a doctrine so sadly abused. Whenever a good man is more than usually weak in the head, he is sure to start a new theory upon Daniel and the Apocalypse. The vagaries of modern prophecy-expositors would be enough to make us utterly sick of all allusion to prophecy were it not that the Lord's Word must ever command our reverence." (1866, 381)

### Nothing but numerals

One of the chief reasons for his dislike of prophecy-exposition was the emphasis upon programmes, diagrams, weird interpretations, dating and so on. When reviewing a book on *Daniel's Mysteries Unveiled* he denounced the book not for its "ingenuity," treating the inspired book of the Bible as "allegory" and the name Daniel a mere "nom de plume," but because he was "all at sea" with the author's "prophetic symbols." For the author it was the importance of "nothing but numerals" rather than the narrative that was important.

## Diagrams and Drawings

With his dislike of relying on the interpretations of numbers went Spurgeon's abhorrence of diagrams. For many years we have referred to prophetic charts as "London tube-stations maps." For Spurgeon they were more reminiscent of Euclid.

Mysterious as the Book of Revelation undoubtedly is, it is far more plain than General Goodwyn's elucidation (the author of the book Spurgeon was reviewing). He writes a pious rigmarole of good things which may have some meaning and connection, but we fail to make out what it is all about. There is a mathematico-prophetical diagram for a frontispiece, which reminded us of Euclid, but the remainder was delusive, for there is nothing demonstrated in the whole book... we wish he would write upon something which he understands." (1877, 186)

Reviewing *Coming Wonders*, he wrote of it as "probably the wildest of all the wild things which the present prophetic mania has produced. This volume of nonsense is adorned with pictures, such as would suit the outside of a travelling show, and its matter will have great weight with the sort of audience which gathered to see ˙Katterfelto and his black cats--Katterfelto with his hair on end at his own wonders, wondering for his bread." (1867, 381)

## Dating and Disappointment

After diagrams and drawings, date-fixing was the next on the list of what annoyed Spurgeon a great deal. After reviewing *The*

---

Note: ˙Katterfelto was an 18th century quack who appeared in London during the influenza epidemic of 1782. He exhibited philosophical apparatus giving microscopic and magnetic demonstrations. George John Whyte-Melville, captain in the Coldstream Guards and a novelist, wrote a novel around Katterfelto in 1875.

*Judgment of Babylon the Great and the Introduction of the Glorious Millennium* by Charles Haddon Spurgeon, he wrote:

> [The author] has put the future in a nutshell, and if we were quite sure that the nut was sound, we should rejoice indeed. We are disappointed to learn that the Jews will be restored in the year 1945, and the Millennium will soon follow, for we shall not live to see it; the author is on the safe side in placing the date beyond the ordinary period of a man's life, for it must be very awkward to survive one's own prophecies, and find them all untrue. (1875, 397)

Notice that he did not condemn or contradict the fact of the author saying that the Jews would be restored to their own land. Some critics of Spurgeon's eschatology deny that Charles Haddon Spurgeon believed this truth. He merely denied the fixing of a date for it.

The author of *The Last Trump* was castigated for his "prophetical declarations... all the signs of the speedy sounding of the last trump, which he sees too clearly in the present state of affairs." Spurgeon commented, "(They) were equally clear to the vision of interpreters 300 years ago, and yet their lucubrations were disproved by time as we venture to believe the intimations of our modern seers will be." (1870, 382)

"So far as the seals are here opened (reviewing a book about *The Revelation of John*), they have often been opened before, and the principle recommendation of the book is that it contains nothing new." Thus he felt "we are doing a good work and cannot come down to them either with sword or the trowel." (1872, 94) As we have said before, he considered his preaching and philanthropic work of primary importance and thus did not enter the fray and preach and write much about eschatological truths.

### Anything and Nothing

From his long experience as an avid reader (since childhood in his grandfather's Manse), and as an inveterate review editor,

Spurgeon knew that the prophetic "experts" could make something out of anything and anything out of nothing. He proved this when reviewing *The Impending Crisis of the Church and the World*. The author having seen, for example, that "the drying-up of the Euphrates referred to the Spanish monarchy (being) overthrown," Spurgeon remarked,

> This is quite enough for us. With such latitude we could find the Eltham murder, the Tichborne Case, the last Derby winner all referred to in the Revelation. We cannot help observing that the more of these prophetical books we are doomed to review, the more sick are we of the entire business. When will men leave the mysterious oracles of God to be interpreted by providence? Their schemes, and outlines, and prognostications dishonour the sacred word from which they profess to draw them. (1871)

They were hardly the words of a die-hard pre-millennialist, for today those of that school of adventist opinions see, or rather saw, when there were ten nations in the Common Market, their Scripture parallel, and in their prophetic magazines still pin-point world events and associate them with events spoken of in the Book of Daniel or The Revelation.

He had no time for such forecasts as "Russia and Austria will descend upon Palestine" or that "America and the colonies of England will assist." Such theories as the English people being the descendants of the ten lost tribes were, in his view, insane, and there was as much evidence for saying that as for saying that "we are descended from the man in the moon and the woman on the halfpenny!" (1877, 43)

When reviewing *The Keys of the Apocalypse* he suggested the author keep his keys "for winding up [his] own watch." If such authors "know so much about the future... it is somewhat odd that they are not able to see four-and-twenty-hours ahead and tell us whether the Turks or the Russians will win on the morrow. (Ibid., 483)

Naturally Charles Haddon Spurgeon was criticized for being so hard on these authors of "prophetical expositions." That was because he loved and revered the Book of Revelation, although "we do not pretend to understand it." He reminded such authors of the third verse of the first chapter: "Blessed is he that readeth." There was, however, "no blessing pronounced on the perusal of commentaries." (1887, 497) He believed "we shall probably understand the Apocalypse itself before we shall be able to comprehend the books which are written to explain it." (1882, 90)

It was Plymouth Brethren writers who annoyed Spurgeon most with their exaggerated claims. He referred to them as "a wandering tribe of religious gipsies... chiefly known as fortune-tellers, practicing the art of necromancy upon the Book of Revelation... decoying members of respectable families of Christian profession away from the homes in which they were born again. (1866, 376)

The above quotation comes from an article in *The Sword and the Trowel* entitled "Jerusalem which is Above." The whole of this article is worth studying in depth in order to assess Spurgeon's eschatological position. For instance, in a footnote he denies the popular Brethren belief of the time in "two comings," something that not all pre-millennialists held to.

**Weird and Wonderful**

Spurgeon could not agree with the dreams, theories and fantasies of the more extreme pre-millennialists. One author he described as suffering from "supposition of the brain," and from reading his book on *Two Years After and Onwards* learned that "Britain is not a 'toe-kingdom' and therefore not to be trodden upon." Regarding the book as a whole he summed it up on the advice Mr. Punch gave to young people thinking of marriage: "Don't," that is, "Don't bother to read it!" (1865, 127)

Of *Things Which Must Shortly Come To Pass: For The Time Is At Hand*, he wrote: "The contents of this little book are about as grotesque as its title." It spoke a great deal about the rapture, and Spurgeon described those bits of information as "reveries," hardly the criticism of a pre-millennialist. In the same way "the political as well as the social outlook is surveyed with some fine touches of fancy." Napoleon was equated with the Antichrist; Poland was to be wrested from Russia, Hungary from Austria, Nice and Savoy from France and so on. All this Charles Haddon Spurgeon saw as a "mingle-mangle" of serious things and "paltry gossip". (1880, 35)

In the same way the author of *The King of Kings and Lord of Lords* sank in "the floods of absurdity, and we cannot attempt to follow him; we look upon his interpretations as wild dreams worthy only of the nursery age of Christian belief." (Ibid, 135)

Perhaps then, it is as well to end with Spurgeon's creedal statement just before he died. Although erroneously called *Mr. Spurgeon's Confession of Faith*, he did not write it--only subscribed to it with twenty-nine other ministers. The last statement of the creed was: "Our hope is the personal pre-millennial return of the Lord Jesus in glory." (1891, 446)

From that statement it is clear that Spurgeon believed that Christ would return to earth before the millennium. From the statements he made in his book reviews it is also clear that he did not believe in the excesses of pre-millennialism as we know it today. But we cannot ear-mark him for any particular escathological school of thought any more than we could in the Calvinistic/Arminian debate. He is not to be ear-marked, pigeon-holed or catalogued in any way. If he had known the twentieth century saying, he would have said that he was his "own man." We cannot fit him into any particular mould, for God made him in His special mould. Not only was he his "own man," but he was God's man--God's man for that particular time in history; God's man whose duty he felt it was to announce truth and denounce error, to preach the gospel of God's grace to sinners and point out to believers the dangers of straying from the paths of Scripture truth.

## CHAPTER FOURTEEN

# Educating and Education

As a small boy, living in his grandfather's manse, Spurgeon was taught to read by his seventeen year old aunt. His primary education was continued when he went to a "dame school," run by a Mrs. Cook in Colchester. When she had taught him as much as she could, he became a pupil at a school run by Mr. Henry Lewis. There, at ten or eleven years of age, he won the First Class English Prize. At fourteen he was sent with his brother to All Saints' Agricultural College, Maidstone. There it was mathematics rather than English in which he shone.

Leaving Maidstone he became an assistant master or junior tutor at John Swindell's School, Newmarket, where he became proficient in Greek, Latin and philosophy, for he was still studying and assisting in the teaching of the younger children. He went on to Cambridge, not to the university, to assist Mr. Leeding, whom he had known when he was an usher in the school of Mr. Henry Lewis.

It seemed as if the young Spurgeon were destined to school-teaching as his life's work, but as we now know, God had other plans. The young educator, however, continued to use his educational gifts in the ministry. Most biographers concentrate on his founding of a college for the training of pastors and missionaries. His mission station Sunday schools and "ragged" schools are given secondary importance, but few deal with the subject of his day school and evening classes.

This is due to the fact that *The Sword and the Trowel* magazine has not been sufficiently researched. The magazines gave regular detailed reports of the Pastor's College, and these are too full to be included here. But his monthly "Notes" also include interesting and little-known facts about his day school and evening classes.

**The Day School**

Spurgeon's day school was founded in 1868 and lasted until 1890 when it became a Board School. A member of the Tabernacle, Mr. S. Johnson, was the master in charge. The school taught grammar, the Bible, history, geography, mental arithmetic, reading, spelling, French, writing, drawing and needlework. It was sited in Station Road, adjoining the Tabernacle's Almshouses. A school-teacher's house was built, and playgrounds were provided.

Spurgeon had written about the proposed project two years before the school was established:

> We have the day school in hand; the ground is purchased, and we hope to give an engraving of the plans in next month's magazine. These are not matters to be done in a day, and we must beg promptness from friends as to their own action, but patience as to our progress, for we have very much in hand. (1866, 418)

No engraving appeared the following month but Spurgeon did make his intentions clearer. Heading his article "Is this Your Business?" he wrote:

> The schools are intended for those of the working classes who desire a good education for their children. It is estimated that an additional £1,000 will be required to furnish the whole cost; this sum will, we have no doubt, be very cheerfully contributed by the friends at the Tabernacle as the works proceed. We have no desire for help in this matter from any friends except our own members and congregation for whose benefit this work will be carried out, and who will, we are confident, very gladly bear their own burden. (Ibid, 479)

The £1,000 was additional to money received from the sale of the New Park Street Chapel, and it can be assumed that it was for the almshouses as well as the day school.

Besides the day school for the children of the working class, he was also hoping to start a Grammar School. He had been making enquiries and had received some promises of aid. A committee of "gentlemen will soon be called together" he promised but needed the promises of parents "willing to send their children to such a school." He was not organizing such a venture for his own gain or glory, rather it was to be an "example and a stimulus to other Dissenters. (Ibid, 480)

He had received a letter for publication in *The Sword and the Trowel*, signed "Testis." That author tried to persuade Spurgeon to found a Nonconformist school for "all classes of Protestant Dissenters" rather than a Baptist school serving Spurgeon's own church. The letter-writer hoped to see, eventually, every county possessing such a grammar school. He had it all worked out, far ahead of Spurgeon, that middle-class schools could be kept going for thirty guineas, and upper schools for those intended for the "learned professions" charging fees of sixty guineas. "Fifty boarders would render each school self-supporting. (Ibid, 474)

In 1867 he could write in the magazine that "by the providence of God one of the schemes laid before our readers a few months ago is now fairly on the way to actual execution." An engraving was at last available and printed in the magazine. It included the almshouses and schoolmaster's house. The work was soon to begin, at a cost of £4,500 and the school would accommodate 200 children. It would be used on Sundays for "Sabbath school." Spurgeon's only regret was that "we cannot make it as large again." (1867, 133 and frontispiece)

Spurgeon's continued interest in the school was not just that of the founder and fund-raiser; he became involved in the academic life of it. On Tuesday, July 7, 1885 he "presided at the public examinations of the scholars in the Day Schools... [and] presented the prizes furnished by himself." In his "Notes" in the magazine he expressed the wish that "we should be glad to see the number of [the] pupils still further increased. We do not think that tradesmen and artisans in the neighborhood of the Tabernacle will find a better school for their children--let them look where they may. It is to us a great pleasure to know that many of the boys have owed their good situations to the solid teaching which they obtained in our Day Schools, and that many of the members of our church had early religious principles instilled and fostered in that institution. (1885, 437)

Later that year he wrote a "Note" saying that "the range of subjects taught is very considerable" and that parents would find it a little more "select" than a Board School. The name of Miss Simpson appears as the teacher of the girls' department; Mr. Johnson remained as head-master. (Ibid, 554)

The following year Spurgeon gave even more explicit details of the success of the school. Quoting from the head-master's report he listed: one girl pupil had been awarded second place out of 200 candidates from all over Great Britain and Ireland for a position in the General Post Office, obtaining only "seven less marks than the candidate who was first." A former pupil had been awarded the position of Special Artist to Guy's Hospital, "selected from among forty applicants." (1886, 554)

Twelve months later he had to write in his magazine that his idea of a grammar school, "a school for the sons of Baptist ministers, similar to that of the Congregationalists at Caterham," had not materialized. Funds had not come in and "so the project has had to remain unborn."

The year before he gave up the idea of his own grammar school he had written of them as an institution in one of his magazine's "Notices of Books." "Suggested Reforms in Public Schools" elicited such criticisms as: Renowned for the soundness of [their classics] and "the severity of their discipline." Then he emphasized the necessity for an all-round education of young people:

> Develop all the faculties, recognizing the fact that boys have muscles as well as brains, and that both need skilful training. Intellectual culture is ill sought to the prejudice of physical health, perennial cheerfulness or manly robustness of moral character. Suggestions on the subject of education still deserve all the time and attention we can afford to bestow on them. The problem is not solved yet. Play has come so much to the front that a reaction is pretty sure to set in. Parents are too proud of their sons' successes at cricket, football, or boat-racing and too little concerned about their proficiency in Latin, Greek, Euclid, and the Sciences. "Cribs" are tolerated in the classes, and "cramming" is practiced for university examinations. We

are averse to both. (1886, 142)

In 1890 Spurgeon had to report:  Our Day School at the Almshouses will be taken over by the School Board for a time, 'till they have built larger premises near the spot. It was useless to hold on with the Board School drawing the children away." (1890, 198) A few months later, reviewing *The Word in the School*, Spurgeon lamented that when Board Schools "were first advocated, we found many Dissenters opposed even to the reading of the Bible in them, and certain of us had to fight a stern battle to secure that minimum of religion--the reading of the Bible." Doubtless from his present vantage point in heaven he sees that the same battle goes on in this twentieth century. And so he went on: "One of these days Christians will wake up to the mournful fact that schools which are not religious are irreligious; and they will begin, at any price, to found schools where the most essential element in education will not be excluded. (Ibid, 451)

Thus ended twenty-two years of provision of religious and comprehensive education for boys and girls. It was not a failure as those few biographers who mention his Day School seem to infer. His ideals are in these present times being adopted by more and more Christian parents who are worried about the secular emphasis their children are receiving under state education.

Spurgeon still had other "irons in the fire" for educating those he knew would appreciate it and benefit from it.

## The Evening Classes

Three years before the start of the monthly magazine, in 1862, Spurgeon began his evening classes in the lecture halls of the Tabernacle. Thus there are no autobiographical notes of the first few years.

The syllabus was designed for teenagers of sixteen and upwards. No fees were charged, and about seventy students began studying from a varied syllabus of science, English language and literature, elementary mathematics and book-keeping. Pitman's shorthand was soon included and each member of the shorthand class was successful in obtaining the

Sir Isaac (Pitman) Elementary Certificate.

Soon the London School Board began to study ways and means of offering evening educational opportunities, and they turned to the Tabernacle for advice. It might be said that Spurgeon was thus the forerunner or the instigator of the London Polytechnic. When in 1899 the Board instituted its own organization then Spurgeon deemed it desirable to discontinue his evening classes at the end of 1899. They had been running for thirty-seven years--fifteen years longer than his day school.

Spurgeon's "Christian Working-Men's College" (as the evening classes became known) ended with over three hundred names on the attendance register. Many of them went on to become members of the Pastor's College without having to begin their course with the drudgery of elementary lessons.

## Education

Nonconformists in general, and Baptists in particular, believed that education should be divorced from the State. As Spurgeon believed in the disestablishment of the Church of England, so he ardently believed that because education at that time included religious education it should not be controlled either by the established Church or the State. In 1833 Parliament voted a grant of £20,000 to be divided between such educational societies as the British and Foreign and the National Society. Many Baptists thought that they should refuse such financial aid from the State. To them it was unscriptural and morally degrading.

The crunch came in 1870, and education became a battle-ground. The Education Act of that year provided a national system of primary schools. The State grant was doubled to Church schools and to Roman Catholic schools. The publicly controlled schools, called Board Schools, had to be supported from local taxes.

Spurgeon joined in the debate when his advice was asked for by Londoners who wished to know how to vote for the first members of the London School Board. He detested the idea that the election should become a contest between established Church and Dissenters. Many disagreed with him and became members of the schools' boards. Those who were ministers were criticized by Charles Haddon Spurgeon for neglecting their churches and turning down preaching engagements. Some, not wishing to fall out of favour with him, refrained from letting their names go forward.

In that critical year (1870) Spurgeon wrote in his magazine Memoranda:

> We trust that all Christians will unite to secure that the Bible be read in all the schools set up by the State. We must have no creeds, or catechisms, or denominational teaching; but there must be liberty for the children to read the Word of God. We propose a conscience clause of a novel order, not one which allows exemption from Bible reading to be claimed as a favour, but which makes the reading of it a privilege to be asked for by those who desire it. Surely no Catholic or Jew or even Secularist can object to this. Religious liberty would be at end if this were not granted. We would counsel Christians to refuse to send their children to the schools if the Bible be excluded; and we believe that if they defied the government compulsion, they would do well. We have long held that the government had better let education alone; but if it must undertake the task, and we think it must, then the utmost freedom must be allowed, and liberty for our children to read the Word of God in the school is one of the rights which no government will have the hardihood to deny, if all Christians unite in demanding it. The Irish school system, and that of the United States are standing instances that the reading of the Bible involves little or no difficulty. (1870, 285)

There is surely food for thought there for each of the three main political parties of today, and also for all Christians, especially those who are turning to the American idea of ACE schools (Accelerated Christian Education) linked with evangelical churches.

One month later he was able to write triumphantly:

The Education Meeting at Exeter Hall over which we presided, was an extraordinary triumph for those who would preserve our national liberties in connection with the proposed new schools. The crowded meeting was made up of working men, and the speakers, all working men, delivered speeches as eloquent as they were brief, which is saying much, for ten minutes was the time allowed to each. When the resolution, that the Bible be permitted to be read in the National Schools by those children whose parents wished it, was put to the meeting, it was carried amid a tumult of cheers, about twenty hands only being held up for the secularist amendment. The working men of London are not prepared to with-hold from their children the book of God. We are amazed that so many religious people should think differently. (Ibid, 332)

Seven years later he was able to write in an even more victorious tone:

When we saw the polling lists for the London School Board we confess that we were as much astonished as delighted. The victory for the undenominational party was so complete, so universal, so far beyond the most sanguine expectations, that we could only look at the list again and again, and then thank God and take courage... moral teaching apart from the Bible we have no faith in, and education without moral teaching will not answer the design which the State aims at, namely, the production of intelligent and orderly citizens. In London we have no question about the use of the Bible in the schools; that is regarded as settled, not only by the authority of the Board, but by the practically unanimous consent of the parents. (1887, 36ff)

As a keen educationalist Spurgeon was interested in, and *au fait* with, all branches of education, from public schools such as Eton, Rugby and Winchester, down to the humble efforts of Victorian governesses. So often we look upon them today as an equivalent of the modern *au pair*, merely someone to act as a "nanny" and perhaps also perform a few household chores. In Spurgeon's day the task of educating the children until ready for private and then public school was in their hands. Even today the Oxford Dictionary defines them as "female teachers, especially of children in a private household."

Ever the philanthropist Spurgeon was keenly away of their working conditions and their future in retirement. Reviewing a book called *A Book for Governesses (by One of Them)* he wrote:

> We always hail with joy any effort to assist this most deserving class of persons, whose lives are frequently full of toil and anxiety, while their old age is, alas! too often embittered by the pangs of want. Few do more for the benefit of others, but though often highly esteemed, we fear they are as often forgotten when the need of their services has passed away. (1869, 42)

Spurgeon himself was a Life Governor of Lewisham Congregational School (his father's alma matter) before it removed to Caterham and later became a Public School. He not only preached the annual sermon on behalf of the school but had the privilege of nine votes to selecting entrants to the school. He was greatly used in improving the educational standards and teaching facilities and boarding amenities of the school, as he was greatly used through his own day schools, evening classes and college. No wonder an early biographer, J. C. Carlile, wrote that "he loved education for its own sake."

CHAPTER FIFTEEN

# 𝕽𝖊𝖛𝖎𝖛𝖆𝖑 𝖆𝖓𝖉 𝕽𝖊𝖓𝖊𝖜𝖆𝖑

So far scholars and biographers have concentrated on Spurgeon's revival sermons, speeches and other addresses. Extracts about revival have been culled from books like *The Bible and the Newspaper* and his commentaries *The Gospel of the Kingdom* and *The Treasury of David*. Little in-depth study has been made of his autobiographical contributions and special articles written for his monthly magazine.

**The Meaning of Revival**

The terms "revival" and "renewal" are often misued. Often "revival" is used when "renewal" would describe the situation better and vice versa. Even the English words carry a sharp distinction, let alone when they are used as theological terms.

"Revival" is to bring back to consciousness, life or existence. "Renewal" is merely to make new or as good as new--to patch up or make young again. The theological sense of the words, as Spurgeon understood them will be seen as we study his writings in *The Sword and the Trowel*. He himself knew both words and experiences. He experienced true revival in his church and frequent renewals; he also perceived it in other churches and upon Great Britain as a whole. He experienced personal revival and then witnessed a Holy Spirit revival upon the New Park Street Chapel.*

---

* For a more detailed study see *Spurgeon on Revival*, Eric Hayden, Zondervan Publishing House, Grand Rapids, 1962, to be reprinted by Pilgrim Publications, Pasadena, TX. Second reprint available in German by J. G. Oncken Verlag Wuppertal und Kassel--*Die Kraft liegt in der Wahrheit: C. H. Spurgeon uber Erweckung.*

Undoubtedly the most important is a six-page article printed in *The Sword and the Trowel* in December 1866. It is entitled "What is a revival?" and in it Spurgeon defines, illustrates and outlines the need for a revival. He admits that for him "the word 'revival' is as familiar in our mouths as a household word." We are constantly speaking about and praying for a revival. He gives the derivation of the words from the Latin: "To live again, to receive again a life which has almost expired; to rekindle into a flame the vital spark which was nearly extinguished."

He gives two illustrations: the restoration of a person who has been rescued from drowning and a young girl returned to consciousness after fainting. "It is clear that the term revival can only be enjoyed by those who have some degree of life. Those who have no spiritual life are not, and cannot be, in the strictest sense of the term, the subjects of a revival." He would thus be at variance with those who equate evangelism with revival. "Many blessings may come to the unconverted in the consequence of a revival among Christians, but the revival itself has to do only with those who already possess spiritual life. There must be vitality in some degree before there can be a quickening of vitality, or, in other words, a revival." Thus "a true revival is to be looked for in the church of God!" He believed, of course, that revival overspilled into the secular world around, but it had to begin with God's people.

**Personal Revival**

What Spurgeon is saying is what the late Edwin Orr said many years later and so many Christians sing lustily, yet without much meaning, in Keswick-type meetings:

O Holy Ghost, revival comes from Thee;
Send a revival--start the work in me:
Thy word declares Thou wilt supply our need;
For blessing now, O Lord, I humbly plead.

Spurgeon expressed it in the beauty of his prose: "It is a sorrowful fact that many who are spiritually alive greatly need reviving." (all above quotations from 1866, 529, 530)

Spurgeon is here repeating what he had said earlier that year when addressing a great united prayer meeting held at the Tabernacle:

> We all of us know that the revival of the whole must be by the revival of each one. Perhaps now will be the time to have a few minutes of silent prayer, in which each heart should seek to draw near to God and make its own petition known, whispering in the ear of the Lord Jesus Christ. (Ibid, 38)

Spurgeon was most concerned that Christian workers knew personal revival. Of ministers of the gospel he wrote: "When a minister obtains this revival he preaches differently from his former manner. It is very hard work to preach when the head aches and when the body is languid, but it is a much harder task when the soul is unfeeling and lifeless. It is sad, sad work-- painfully, dolorously, horribly sad, but saddest of all if we do not feel it to be sad, if we can go on preaching and remain careless concerning the truths we preach, indifferent as to whether men are saved or lost! May God deliver every minister from abiding in such a state! (1866, 532) He likened such a preacher to "a mere signpost, pointing out the road but never moving in it. (Ibid)

Elders and deacons also needed personal revival, for "what different men it would make of them!" He knew that "lifeless, lukewarm church officers are of no more value to a church than a crew of sailors would be to a vessel if they were all fainting and ill in their berths when they were wanted to hoist the sails or lower the boats. Church officers who need reviving must be fearful dead weights upon a Christian community." While he expected all believers "to be thoroughly awake to the interests of Zion," he urged that "special supplication should be made for beloved brethren in office that they may be full of the Holy Ghost." (Ibid)

So it should be with "Sunday-school [workers], tract distributors, and other labourers for Christ, what different people they become when grace is vigorous from what they are when their life flickers in the socket!" (Ibid, 532 533)

When ordinary believers "are revived they live more consistently, they make their homes more holy and more happy, and this leads the ungodly to envy them, and to enquire their secret." (Ibid)

What then was his secret for such personal revival in preachers and for those who occupy the pews?

## Revival and Doctrine

We speak of "vital godliness," and vital godliness must subsist upon vital truth. Vital godliness is not revived in Christians by mere excitement, by crowded meetings, by the stamping of the foot, or the knocking of the pulpit cushion, or the delirious bawlings of ignorant zeal; these are the stock in trade of revivals among dead souls but to revive the living saints other means are needed. (Ibid, 532)

Well said! If only they could be widely broadcast in our present-day climate of charismatic excitement with "holy" laughter, slaying in the Spirit, dancing in the aisles and all the other excesses of the "New Wave" from America. No wonder Spurgeon went on: "Intense excitement may produce a revival of the animal, but how can it operate upon the spiritual, for the spiritual demands other food than that which stews in the fleshpots of mere carnal enthusiasm. The Holy Ghost must come into the living heart through living truth, and so bring nutriment and stimulant to the pining spirit, for so only can it be revived." (Ibid)

This is one point on which he agreed with Charles Finney. Reviewing *Lectures to Professing Christians*, he said that he did not doubt his faith and zeal and realized his previous book, *Lectures on Revivals of Religion*, had produced "considerable sensation" and had "had their influence upon subsequent revivals." His latter book, however, was "more in harmony with those of 'like precious faith,'" and he was "at one" with Finney when he stated: "You must bring the sinner to see that he is entirely dependent on free grace; and that full and complete justification is bestowed on the first act of faith as a mere gratuity, and no part of it as an equivalent for anything he is to do. This alone dissolves the influence of selfishness, and secures holy action." (1877, 282)

As to the other doctrines of grace that needed to be preached to produce a genuine revival, especially the "five points" of Calvinism, they are dealt with in *Spurgeon on Revival* and refer us to his sermons rather than his *Sword and the Trowel*.

## The Holy Spirit and Revival

As well as correct doctrine there had to be the work of the Holy Spirit if a true revival was to be wrought in the believer's soul. Writing in *What is a Revival?* Spurgeon continued:

> If we are to obtain a revival we must go directly to the Holy Ghost for it, and not resort to the machinery of the professional revival-maker. The true vital spark of heavenly flame comes from the Holy Ghost, and the priests of the Lord must beware of strange fire. There is no spiritual vitality in anything except as the Holy Spirit is all in all in the work; and if our vitality has fallen near to zero, we can only have it renewed by Him who first kindled it in us. (1866, 532)

Worldliness Spurgeon saw as one of the chief reasons for a Christian's state of lethargy that needed reviving by the Holy Spirit:

> When a man has been let down into a vat or into a well full of bad air, you do not wonder when he is drawn up again that he is half-dead, and urgently requires to be revived. Some Christians--to their shame be it spoken-- descend into such worldly company, act upon such unhallowed principles, and become so carnal, that when they are drawn up by God's grace from their backsliding position they want reviving, and even need that their spiritual breath should as it were be breathed into their nostrils afresh by God's Spirit. (Ibid, 530)

Sometimes he referred to the work of the Holy Spirit as "a heavenly visitation." Reviewing *A Narrative of the Great Revival*

*Work in South Wales in 1871* he called it "a very gracious work (the revival not the book)... a heavenly visitation." (1872, 91) As to the book itself it was "calculated to do good and to arouse in our sleepy churches a desire for" such a visitation from on high. (Ibid)

## Children and Revival

Charles Haddon Spurgeon was very keen on child conversion. His little booklet, produced from a sermon entitled "Come ye Children," is a classic and has helped many a Sunday school teacher. He was just as emphatic about the place of children in revivals. Reviewing a book *Handbook of Revivals: for the use of Winners of Souls*, he called it "a judicious compilation from almost every work upon the subject of revivals, and is written in a spirit calculated to promote them." The author was Dr. Henry Fish. Spurgeon had already given an extract from the book, *Singing in Revivals* in a previous issue of his magazine, but in January 1875 he emphasised the importance of children in times of revival. The extract was about a sick girl of ten years of age who had a firm belief in Jesus Christ for salvation. Dr. Fish listed several cases of revival affecting children: "a prayer-room where many little ones were praying... the work of God," was one that influenced the thinking of an eminent Scotch minister. The author concluded with a quotation from McCheyne: "Jesus has reason to complain of us that He can do no mighty works in our Sunday-schools because of our unbelief." (1875, 40)

## The Revival Year

Spurgeon spoke and wrote of the year 1872 as *Revival Year* or *The Year of Grace*. It was his opening article in *The Sword and the Trowel* for January 1872 and set out his expectations and prayers for the ensuing twelve months. He began: "There is a great need for a season of revival among the churches, and we have personal reason to believe that it is coming. If it be the Lord's will, a gracious time of refreshing will occur, and we think we have good warrant for anticipating it."

The grounds for his expectations were: the influence of his printed sermons at home and abroad, on land and on sea; a spontaneous prayer meeting on a Monday evening among his elders--"a work of God;" two days of sitting in his vestry to deal with anxious souls--"they streamed in all day;" another time had to be arranged to deal with the "more than two hundred and fifty seekers;" on the second occasion between 400 and 500 were present and "the attention was almost oppressive to the pastor's soul." These last examples were not the result of exciting evangelistic methods: "there was not even the shadow of excitement... all was quiet." (1872, 1ff)

## Objections to Revival

He encountered objections, naturally, some from national newspapers like *The Times*. He answered them in his usual forthright manner in *The Sword and the Trowel*. With some of the newspaper objections he was in agreement, especially that of spasmodic efforts against a "continuous revival" and the "abiding power" of true preachers like Whitefield and Wesley. He also agreed that many revival meetings were too long and went on too far into the night, yet "Nobody has written to the papers to complain that his daughters stayed at an evening party after ten o'clock or that his son came home a little before eleven from the opera. There is a deal of cant in the irreligious world, and its hypocrisies are innumerable. That once in a while a meeting should be protracted beyond the hour allowed by prudence is not so great a sin after all." (1874, 138)

The main thrust of *The Times* article was against "the excitement engendered." With this Spurgeon partly agreed, but added:

> We have never heard either Liberal or Conservative argue in this manner. Men grow eager in the pursuit of wealth, and the pulse beats fast when great transactions are quivering in the balance; the world does not blame them

for this, for it thinks the object of their pursuit worthy of intense effort: but if a man grows earnest in seeking the salvation of his soul, he is censured for being too excited, and if he weeps for his sins, or rejoices when he has obtained pardon for them, he is set down at once as being under the influence of fanatics and his confinement in Bedlam is confidently predicted. (Ibid)

Today he would probably have instanced Wimbledon or the World Cup to compare the world's excitement with the excitement engendered in a spiritual revival. Of the latter he said, "Nothing... in holy Scripture can be urged against the legitimate use of excitement in religion. It is to the largest degree a business of the heart; we say to the largest degree because we do not deny that it is a matter of the understanding, the memory, and all the other faculties of the mind, and surely if the heart preponderates there must be a measure of excitement." (Ibid, 139)

He concluded his article by writing:

We deprecate solemnly the excesses of certain revivalists; we lament the foolish rant and false doctrines which have poisoned former movements in certain quarters; but our solemn conviction is that the present gracious visitation which many parts of England and Scotland are enjoying is of the Lord, and should be hailed with delight by all gracious men. God speed it. (Ibid)

He not only expected a measure of excitement to accompany a revival but also "deep and extensive anxiety for the welfare of the church, and for the glory of God in the salvation of man." He believed there was no hope of a revival when believers were "stolid" and had no "vehement desire for souls." (1872, 373ff)

There also had to be a spirit of expectancy among God's people; Christian workers must be expecting a revival at all times. We are to be like watchmen, "expecting to announce the signs which light up the sky." (Ibid) But, "such signs may not be much valued, nay, will not be recognized by the mere professor; but, to the man whose soul is all aglow with the divine fire, whose mind is on the wing and ready to hail the faintest trace of springtime in the church of the living God, such signs are like unto salvation. Despise not the faintest sign; for, as the modest flower, peeping out from behind the snows of winter, announces the approaching spring, so a single conversion, or one earnest heart, may be the beginning of a fruitful season--the first sign of revival." (Ibid)

May Spurgeon's God and our God keep us on our spiritual toes eagerly and excitedly looking for the signs of a time of refreshing from the presence of the Lord.

## CHAPTER SIXTEEN

# 𝕸𝖊𝖘𝖘𝖆𝖌𝖊𝖘 𝖆𝖓𝖉 𝕸𝖆𝖌𝖆𝖟𝖎𝖓𝖊𝖘

Little did Spurgeon realize, when he issued his first *Penny Pulpit* or printed weekly sermon, that after his lifetime it would become the largest collection of sermons in the English-speaking world. Beginning with *The New Park Street Pulpit* (six volumes) and continuing with *The Metropolitan Tabernacle Pulpit* (fifty-seven volumes), these sixty-three volumes are still being reprinted today. They contain altogether 3,563 separate sermons, many of them issued in various translations.

A Welsh sermon was the first to appear and was published once a month. The Queen of Holland requested copies of the Dutch editions. There were others in Arabic, Bengali, Chinese, Danish, Estonian, French, German, Hungarian, Italian, Japanese, Kaffir, Lettish, Maori, Norwegian, Polish, Russian, Spanish, Tamil and Urdu, just to give one instance from nearly each letter of the alphabet. Both Moon and Braille type was issued for the blind.

Dr. A. T. Pierson once calculated that no less than ten thousand men and women had been saved through the reading of the sermons alone. Yet they have been analyzed and criticised detrimentally by many.

The author had passed on to him many original volumes by his grandfather and father. The earliest of his grandfather's contained the date 1879 on the flyleaf. As he was joint-superintendent of the Orphanage Sunday School for fifty-four years, beginning in 1880, it is hardly likely he was given that position after being a Tabernacle member for just one year. He must have "sat under" Spurgeon some years prior to 1879, possibly from 1874 when he left Essex and came to London. These original volumes of sermons the author sent to a Czechoslovakian pastor each time he received his new edition. The pastor's country was then still under Communist rule, yet each volume got through and was "devoured" by the pastor. It was well-worth losing the originals to encourage and bless such a man.

In spite of the criticism of his sermons by contemporaries and Christian and non-Christian press, what did Charles Haddon Spurgeon himself think of his own printed messages? No one seems to have delved into the magazine "Notes" to discover what Spurgeon's reaction was to their wide acceptance throughout the Continent and then countries in various parts of the world. He was always so thrilled to hear about his printed sermons from missionaries and visitors from the nations into whose language they had been translated. There is sufficient material in *The Sword and the Trowel* for someone to collect them into a book as this present author has done with the conversion stories printed in his magazine.

### Regular Readers

Many of the reports Spurgeon received about the spiritual response to his printed sermons were about those who had read them "by chance" or "accidentally," as they thought. Charles Haddon Spurgeon would never have used those terms, for as a Calvinist he believed such chance encounters were predestined and ordained. Many others, of course, after buying the first sermon became regular readers--some for many, many years.

Such was the "poor old needlewoman, a godly soul." As she could not get out to the services much she was advised by a Christian lady who was visiting her to read Spurgeon's sermons "for her comfort and joy." The needlewoman replied that she had been reading them for the past twenty years, even though at the end of the week she was left with just "three pence to carry her on until Monday." She spent the three pence thus: "ld. sermon, ld. bread, and ld. tea." Then she added, "I would not have changed places with the Queen when I got into the cream of the sermon, and I often forgot to eat my bread."

When she had accumulated a number of sermons, "although

+ *He Won Them For Christ: 30 Conversions Under Spurgeon's Ministry*, Eric Hayden, Christian Focus Publications Ltd., Fearn, Ross-shire, Scotland, 1993.

a feeble soul," she went about distributing them in order that other people might share the blessing that had come to her through reading them. (1881, 293, 294)

Another regular reader, a minister in St. Petersburg, had a friend in that city who passed his on "to an old Russian pope," who in turn passed them on to other priests. The minister himself knew of several priests in the city and the interior who were regular readers. (Ibid)

**Telling Translation**

The above minister in St. Petersburgh told Spurgeon how the Russian censor often gave permission for his sermons to be translated when other people's sermons were denied that privilege. Most countries were more than willing to translate them. In France the little monthly paper, *L'Echo de las Verite*, included a translation of sermon No. 1,500 to be published in England. Spurgeon received the report about the French paper while he was recuperating at Menton from an illness. He commented in his magazine "Personal Notes:" "It is exceedingly appropriate that in this manner [he] should now be daily speaking to the French in their own tongue whilst enjoying the benefit of their sunny shores." (1880, 90)

One translation into French was very striking, for it was not authorized by Spurgeon himself, indeed he was unaware of it until some time later. The incident is so intriguing that it must be recounted in full as given in *The Sword and the Trowel*:

> In 1866, Mr. Spurgeon came to Paris, and, as he could not preach in French, many of my [missionary clergyman] friends, who had gone long distances to hear him, were disappointed. At the request of a good many of my own congregation and other friends, I went to Paris, and took copious notes of the different sermons. When I returned I was pressed to give these sermons in French. When it became known that I was to do so, great crowds came to hear me. By way of introduction I just asked them for the time to fancy I was Mr. Spurgeon, as I wished to try and

deliver them with the same effect as he had done.

A few years after that a lady called on me, and wished to be admitted as a member of the Protestant Church of which I was the pastor. I asked her what had led her to think of this. She replied that a few years ago that she, along with other Roman Catholics, had gone to hear a man who had been in Paris, and was to give a translation of Spurgeon's sermons. She followed closely the sermon from the text, "I am the good Shepherd" and had thus been awakened. (1882, 98, 99)

Spurgeon was "greatly refreshed [in] spirit)" when a nobleman of Alsace visited him at Menton and gave him copies of two of his sermons which he had translated into French, "lithographed in running hand," to be read in congregations. We found our friend almost as well acquainted with our work as if he had attended the Tabernacle all his life." (1879, 294) This was another unauthorized translation that had a most telling effect, as if it had been issued from a French publishing house.

## Missionary Messages

One day at Menton Mr. Broomhall, home affairs director of Hudson Taylor's mission, visited Spurgeon with a copy of his sermon "The Divine Call for Missionaries." It was scored and underlined, and "had been carried about in his pocket by a brother who is now a missionary; the sermon having constrained him to devote himself to that work for the Lord." No wonder Spurgeon added in his Personal Matters column: "We prized that discourse more than if the princes of the land had covered it with jewels. To God be the glory." (Ibid)

Further testimony to the usefulness of Spurgeon's missionary sermon was given in the magazine of the China Inland Mission, *China's Millions*. It was an extract from a missionary's letter which the secretary of the C. I. M. had received. It stated: "There are [now] three working in connection with the C. I. M. who are led to give themselves for the work in China through Mr. Spurgeon's sermon." (1881, 490)

Sometimes readers themselves became missionaries after reading a sermon by Spurgeon. The testimony of a Swiss lady was that her parents were members of the Protestant Established Church in Switzerland. The daughter "attended the ordinances, and observed the ceremonies." She felt a hypocrite since she did not whole-heartedly believe in them. Coming to England she read a sermon by Spurgeon "which did me good... I then bought his sermons and read them, and I am now happy to say that I am trusting in Jesus. When I get home I shall distribute these sermons which have been so blessed to me." (Ibid)

Missionaries in the sense of city missioners and colporteurs also used the sermons to great effect in their visitation. One fisherman in Scotland remembered a colporteur visiting his parents house, and he answered the door. Asked to buy a book he said he would if it were a book of Scotch songs. The colporteur said: "If you give me a piece of fish I will give you something that will do you more good than ballads." He gave the fisherman a Spurgeon's sermon and received in exchange half a cod-fish. The text was, "Look unto me and be ye saved, all the ends of the earth: for I am God, and there is none else." While reading the sermon "the blessed Spirit of God enlightened [his] understanding, and [he] saw Jesus set before [him] as [his] Saviour." He expressed his joy in the words, "Happy day! Jesus washed my sins away." (Ibid)

### Remarkable Results

The examples above are all remarkable, but some results from his sermons that Spurgeon heard about were extraordinary in the way the sermons came to people's attention, let alone the spiritual result they achieved.

One lady wrote to Spurgeon telling how her unsaved nephew in Wales was sent a newspaper from Australia. It contained a sermon by Spurgeon on "The Wicked Man's Life, Funeral, and Epitaph." It was the means of the man's conversion, the sermon having begun in London, gone out to Australia, and on it's return trip from the other side of the world reached man's sinful need back in Great Britain.

Another woman was shopping in Christchurch when she lost her purse containing £6 14s. She had some handbills printed and circulated offering a reward for the restoration of her property. Someone found the purse but stole the money. Some time later a man visited the printer of the handbills and asked for particulars about the incident. He asked the printer to return the purse to its rightful owner, asking no questions. Inside was the original sum plus £3 interest. "The cause which brought this about was reading Spurgeon's sermons." (1881, 587)

A death-bed confession was perhaps one of the most remarkable incidents told about these sermons. It appeared in the American edition of the *Christian Herald* and was sent to Spurgeon from their New York office. The editor wrote:

> I think it will cheer you to learn that we have recently heard of some remarkable cases, in which very wicked and desperate men have given up their revolvers and bowie knives, and have become like children in spirit, through the blessing of God on your sermons published in our columns. One aged reprobate, sixty years old, died last week, whose last two years were in startling contrast to all his past life. The transformation was the wonder of the neighbourhood for its completeness. From being a public terror he became a blessing, as gentle and as kind as a woman. He was delivered from drunkenness, profanity, unchastity, and blood-shedding. On his death-bed he desired that you should be told of this, as he owed his conversion, under God, to a sermon of yours which he read in a stray copy of the *Christian Herald*, which some one brought into the Ranch and left behind. He quaintly said that "he should tell Jesus about you." (1884, 200)

## Preacher's Plagiarism

Spurgeon was fond of telling the story of how he was on holiday and went to a small country church and heard one of his own sermons read word for word. Afterwards the young minister, too busy to write his own that week, realized who his renowned visitor was and blushed to the roots of his hair. Spurgeon graciously told him how much one of his own sermons was just what he needed on that occasion and how much it had helped him.

That unknown plagiarist was not alone in cribbing one of the Prince of Preachers' messages. Spurgeon once recounted in his magazine "Notes" how he had learned from a minister in North America how great was his influence in that country. Not only were "Baptists out here... praying for Mr. Spurgeon as a special duty... I have also discovered that preachers of other denominations are using these sermons, from introduction to conclusion, and after the service it is somewhat amusing to find the volume under the seat of the sleigh." (1880, 242)

Perhaps it was better to use a sermon by Spurgeon and see conversions than use a home-made one and see nothing. At any rate, the preacher at the Metropolitan Tabernacle did not object to the practice; rather he rejoiced in this further influence of the printed word.

It is good to know that the practice has not died out. The present author is in contact from time to time with a painter-and-decorator who bought a complete set of *The Metropolitan Tabernacle Pulpit* (reprinted in America) in order to read them to the crofters in the Highlands of Scotland, something that was done when they were originally printed and published. With the discovery of north-sea oil off the coast of Scotland it meant that the influx of workers gave a fillip to this man's decorating business, and he was able to afford the outlay necessary for a complete set of sermons. Eternity alone will reveal the continuing blessing from Spugeon's printed messages.

## Food and Drink

For isolated people like crofters and lonely people like the shut-ins of Victorian times, Spurgeon's sermons became their spiritual food and drink. Unable to get to church through illness, disability, or long distance, the weekly sermon was their spiritual sustenance. Through them they were converted; through them they grew in grace and in a knowledge of Jesus Christ. A remarkable instance of this occurred in America and was listed in *One Thousand New Illustrations for Pulpit, Platform, and Class* which Spurgeon reviewed in *The Sword and the Trowel*. There were one thousand illustrations in the collection and Spurgeon referred to our example as "a good instance." The incident illustrated "inconsistency." This is it in its entirety:

> The captain of a vessel, captured in the Amercian war, was courteously offered by his captor permission to bring away his personal effects. He made a most ludicrous scene by earnestly appealing that he might be allowed to take with him Spurgeon Sermons and a keg of very fine whiskey. The sermons were granted, but he was told that the whiskey must go overboard. (1887, 638)

Visitors to France in a similar situation to Spurgeon, there for health reasons and recuperating after illness, often found it difficult to find a place of worship where the services were in English. Thus spiritual food was often denied them until their return to England. Besides being a preacher to multitudes Spurgeon never minded speaking to small numbers. He would invite a small congregation to his hotel and then set before them as rich a fare as he would have given if he had been ministering at home in his vast Tabernacle. By printing the message afterwards in *The Sword and the Trowel* he ensured a wider public were fed at a subsequent date.

In the February 1880 issue he printed "a sermon preached in his own room at Menton to an audience of fourteen friends." The title of the sermon was "The Pearl of Patience" (James 5:11), and his select congregation were fed on a diet of Job's patience--"a man like ourselves, imperfect and full of infirmity," "a greatly tried man," "a man who endured up to the very end" and "one who thereby has become a great power for good." Leaving Job and turning to the Lord, Spurgeon's second course of the meal consisted of "the Lord was in it all," "the Lord was blessing Job by his tribulation" and "the Lord in mercy brought him out of it all with unspeakable advantage." What rich fare for "afflicted saints" as he called them. "He who tested with one hand supported with the other." (1880, 49ff)

For a handfull in a hotel room it was a delightful picnic, for thousands of magazine readers it was a two course (with appetiser before and coffee afterwards) meal, spiritual food and drink perhaps for a whole month until the next issue of the magazine appeared.

During that time Spurgeon was not idle. He appealed in his magazine while resting at Menton for his readers to remember that "we have more than enough to do during our rest to keep us from rust. Among the "unconsidered trifles" is the bringing out of the weekly sermon. This costs us a fair day's work. We issue the sermon week by week, wherever we may be, and as we have no goods of this sort laid up for many days, we have the work to do in the same way as at home." (1887, 598)

And what was true for the weekly sermons was also true for the monthly magazine; these too he attended to when away from home.

### The Magazines

As he could not have forseen how the sermons would become more and more popular after his lifetime, so he knew little of the future of the magazine he started in 1865. He began and continued with great courage, not "in a timid, crouching spirit, neither have we pandered to popular tastes. Some of our articles have brought down upon us upbraidings which we have borne without regret. Our reviews, when we have felt conscientiously bound to censure, have cost us many a postal lecture. We are not, however, penitent; we have nothing to retract, but doubt not that we shall sin again... We use the trowel wherever we can to aid every good cause, but we have a sword also and mean to use it." (1870, iii)

### Aim and Object

On printing one of his sermons in the magazine, *A Sermon on a Grand Old Text* (I Timothy 1:15), he added this footnote: "Our one aim and object in conducting this magazine is the glory of God in the saving of sinners, the building up of his church and the slaying of error. We insert details of good works in order to stimulate workers for Jesus, but we feel that the magazine must also itself aim at conversions. To that end, we insert this sermon, as well as other articles of like character." (1872, 293)

Beginning the second decade of publication he reminded readers in his Preface that Christian magazines should not be "made up of pious platitudes, heavy discourses and dreary biographies of nobodies: the Sabbath literature of our families might be as vivacious and attractive as the best amusing serials, and yet as deeply earnest and profitable as the soundest of divines would desire... true to our coat of arms, *The Sword and the Trowel*, we have smitten here and there with such force as the case required and our arm allowed, and we have builded upon the wall with some measure of diligence." (1875, iiii)

As time went by and he saw the error creeping in to the Baptist and other non-conformist denominations, he wrote: "There is sad need to keep the sword out of its scabbard, for the enemy is gathering strength, and mustering his bold forces for fiercer attacks. What doctrine is now left unassailed? What holy thing is regarded as sacred? Truths once regarded as fundamental, are either denied, or else turned inside out till nothing of their essence remains. Holy Scripture is no longer admitted to be the infallible record of revelation; but is made to be a door-mat for thought to wipe its shoes upon." (1883, iii)

Where is there such a magazine today when the same doctrinal errors are with us? There are those who try to emulate Spurgeon but only succeed in knocking down and not building up. Their sword is drawn but their trowel is disused. The amazing thing about *The Sword and the Trowel* is that it was an "in-house" magazine, giving encouraging reports of the work of Spurgeon's many evangelistic and philanthropic agencies, yet at the same time as describing "labour for the Lord" it engaged in "combat with sin." Through articles, sermons, Bible commentary and book reviews, it provided thousands of Christians with food for thought and much prayer fodder.

### Proof-reading and Readership

Twelve years after its beginning Spurgeon wrote in the

Preface: "We trust that the matter and style of *The Sword and the Trowel* have not deteriorated, for we have spared no pains, and have read every line carefully ourselves." (1876, iv)

This he said, or wrote, in various ways at different times, especially when recuperating in the south of France. He besought readers not to occupy his time with invitations to preach and other correspondence as his time was fully taken up with sermons to be corrected and proofs of the magazine to be read. Besides which he wanted to rest and get better. On one occasion a friend said in his hearing that "as for the magazine, it was a merely nominal thing to be the editor, for few editors ever saw their magazines until they were in print." Spurgeon replied, "However this may be as a rule, it does not contain a spark of truth in my case, for I have personally superintended every page, and I do not think a single line of the magazine has passed through the press without having been read by me. Whether I succeed or not, I certainly do not delegate my task to others." (1881, iii)

From Menton he began one month's "Notes" by saying that he had "carefully prepared and arranged every page of the present magazine, and sent it forth with the best wishes for the New Year to all friends and readers. (1884, 42)

Who were these "friends and readers" besides his church members and loyal congregation? Ministers not only of Baptist persuasion but from every other denomination, non-conformist, established church and Roman Catholic, were avid readers. But sometimes the most unlikely people read *The Sword and the Trowel*. Everybody thinks that the Salvation Army officer who sells *The War Cry* in public houses has the monopoly. In fact Spurgeon's magazine was also purchased in pubs. Spurgeon noted in June 1878 that "the London City Missionary in the public-houses of Walworth writes to say that many coffee-houses in his district are supplied with *The Sword and the Trowel* monthly, and he adds, 'These are highly prized by the proprietors and very many of their customers, and I believe much good is thus done in a quiet, unostentatious manner. Neither the proprietors nor I know who pays for them, but I am told, a kind lady leaves them every month.'" (1878, 318)

When *The Sword and the Trowel* was reviewed by another

publication it had a good write-up and was described as "vivacious and good," and that "notwithstanding the absence of the editor." Spurgeon was quick to reply:

> "The editor is never absent from the magazine; but personally reads every line of each number. Friends now and then write, blaming some supposed subordinate, if their tastes are not pleased; but the editor hides behind nobody, friends must blame him, for he is personally responsible. Our writers are able men, and are quite able to fight their own battles, should battles occur; but the editor never wishes it to be imagined that he merely puts his name on the cover of the magazine, and leaves it to be produced by other people... Notwithstanding illness, or absence from home, we have never been obliged to delegate our duties to anyone else; on the contrary, we have given all the more time to this work when we have been debarred from other labours." (1885, 194)

In "Notices of Books" in 1882 Spurgeon reviewed volume 17 of *The Sword and the Trowel*, and in his review emphasised that second-hand volumes "fetched good prices," which he considered "about as good a test of literary value as we can give." He also listed the sort of readers devoted to the magazine: "not only... among our own denomination of Christians, but among the clergy of other churches and residents in foreign lands." (1882, 33)

Not only was some of his readership from the Church of England but also wealthy. It was through the magazine that "the Stockwell Orphanage originated," and we know that an Anglican lady, Mrs. Anne Hillyard, became the original benefactor to so many children. After reading an article by Spurgeon in his magazine, *The Holy War of the Present Hour*, she sent him a cheque for £20,000. No wonder *The Sword and the Trowel* logo was built into the original orphanage building. (1881, iii)

After completing its twenty-second year of "doing practical work for the King," the magazine "must be pretty good," said Spurgeon, for "almost every article is reprinted by some paper or other, and we come across our paragraphs in publications which do not acknowledge their source." (1886, iii) That did not mean that it was never criticized. In 1883 the Bishop of Rochester severely criticized Spurgeon's publication, and Charles Haddon Spurgeon printed the Bishop's speech to the House of Lords in which he described the magazine as "a lively newspaper." Spurgeon denied that it was a "newspaper" but insisted that it was a monthly periodical. Since the Bishop's criticism arose out of the matter of church lands and the number of public houses built on them, Spurgeon took the opportunity once again of stressing the need for disestablishment. He also denied that his magazine article had anything to say on the subject of church lands and public houses. His friend Canon Wilberforce had seen the article and wrote to the Archbishop of Canterbury in defense of Spurgeon.

To mark twenty-five years of producing *The Sword and the Trowel* Spurgeon stated, "We shall adopt a new wrapper... there will be no change in its doctrine, nor in its method of promoting it. Our colours are nailed to the mast." (1889, iii) That silver-jubilee year of the magazine was to be the penultimate year of his earthly life and ministry, but as we look back we can see that he was always true to his aims and object, even to "this magazine contains the material for its editor's biography or at least for the story of his work." (1886, iv) What a pity, then, that more research has not been done into this mine of information in order that a definitive biography might be offered to the Christian public.

## CHAPTER SEVENTEEN

# Suffering and Healing

Charles Haddon Spurgeon suffered for most of his life and for all of his ministerial life. When he wrote an autobiographical article in March 1890 for *The Sword and the Trowel* on the occasion of his preaching in the Surrey Gardens Music Hall, he said that on seeing the crowds waiting for him "[he] felt overawed, and was taken with that faintness which was, in [his] youth, the usual forerunner of every sermon." (1890, 110) The ministerial life in general, and preaching in particular, was something that had to be paid for in physical weakness, mental distress and spiritual anguish.

Often his painful physical condition "turned [his] smooth and sunny seas into tempestuous deeps," but with resignation he realized that "it is clear we must both serve and suffer; and we ask for grace to do both in the best manner." He drew an analogy with his own magazine: "Labouring with diligence, and enduring with patience, it will be *The Sword and the Trowel* again in another fashion." (1887, 41) Changing the figure of speech the following year, he used the illustration of a ship on a stormy sea, the sea of life: "We are not wrecked, but have seen the works of the Lord, and his wonders in the deep. Long has our motto been, 'I have chosen thee in the furnace of affliction,' and it proves itself to be true." Even in suffering he was a Calvinist. He saw his suffering as part of the sovereign God's plan for his life. This, however, did not solve the practical problems of suffering: we cannot get better until we are in another climate, and we cannot reach that other climate till we get better." (1888, 651)

His Calvinism comes out when replying in *The Sword and the Trowel* to a doctor's criticism of his theology of suffering in *Christian World*. Spurgeon had expressed the view that his painful and prolonged rheumatism was the result of "the mistral at Marseilles" but was also "of the Lord's sending." He described the wind as "the scourge of Provence, and is neither the friend of fruits nor flowers, but is regarded as the enemy of man, beast, and plant." But even if the wind was not sent to encourage the growth of vegetation, Spurgeon believed that did not prevent it "answering other divine purposes as well... While winds blow for great, far-reaching purposes, the infinite Jehovah also sends them for special and individual designs... The fact that wind and weather can be scientifically predicted and that they are produced by fixed laws we know quite as well as M. D.; we are quite scientific enough for that, but this by no means opposes the grand doctrine that the hand of the Lord ordereth all things. Fixed laws do not operate apart from divine power... we trust we are not less reverent and scientific when we behold God in everything than those who see Him only here and there... Though He slay us, yet will we trust Him. We loathe the very idea of calling our God vindictive." (1877, 189)

Biographers write of his suffering in terms of "kidney disease," "Bright's disease," "gout," "depression" and so on. In the year before he died he wrote an article for his magazine with three question marks as the title--"???". In it he described his "long, wasting sickness," "feebleness," a "murmur," "leakage of life power," his "serious condition." (1891, 645ff) These are not the medical and more detailed terms that he used in earlier bulletins given in *The Sword and the Trowel* during his Tabernacle ministry. From those it is clear that his suffering was of a threefold kind, *physical, mental* (or emotional and nervous) and *spiritual*. In 1884 he summed up his condition in these words: "Every limb of my body is tormented with pain; there is about as much pain in each limb an any one of them can conveniently bear. In addition to this, the whole system, mind and body, is in a state of fidgets, *malaise,* and depression." (1884, iii)

## Physical pain

Gout is medically acknowledged as a very painful disease. Today's drugs were not available in Spurgeon's time, and so the suffering was even more painful. Thus he would frequently write in his monthly magazine "Notes:" "[The editor] unhappily took a chill, which was followed by gout... he is still confined to his bed and suffering greatly." Asking correspondents not to write for preaching engagements he said, "It is a great aggravation of his pains when he has to refuse requests for services which he is utterly unable to render. (1891, 417)

At other times it was neuralgia that took its toll and kept him from his pulpit and sent him away from home to recuperate. He described this condition as "day after day of wretched pain, and golden hours lost in miserable incompetence." (1885, 645)

The London fogs in winter brought about physical weakness, forcing him to seek the warmer climate of southern France. One result of fog in the Metropolis was voice trouble. After preaching "every Lord's day for about seven months... a weakness has happened to our voice on several occasions... but the fogs of November warn us that our time for holiday has fully come. To continue at [our] post, even when in weakness and measurable pain, is the preacher's earnest endeavour, and friends may rest assured that [we] will never be absent while [we are] able to hold on." (1890, 537)

## Mental distress

Today doctors know that the physical affects the nervous system and vice-versa. In Spurgeon's day the two were often separated, and a person who was physically ill did not always have the nervous tension behind it fully assessed. A great deal of Spurgeon's physical suffering would today be considered as having a nervous origin. This was especially true of his depression.

It was not merely depression that dogged him mentally and emotionally and nervously. In 1891, when constant physical weakness was bringing about his early demise, he had to record: "For the first time in a ministry of forty years, we entered the pulpit on the Sunday evening, and were obliged to hurry out of it; for a low, nervous condition shut us up." (1891, 347) This inability to face his congregation may have been a "one-off" for Charles Haddon Spurgeon, but for many a lesser mortal it has been a frequent occurrence during a difficult pastorate. The late Dr. D. Martyn Lloyd-Jones often counselled younger ministers with the very same problem and once told the present writer that a Christian headmistress had the same problem when facing her morning assembly.

The peak of Spurgeon's mental anguish was during the *Down-Grade Controversy,* and in 1888 he published a doctor's certificate in his monthly "Notes:"

> This is to certify that Mr. Spurgeon is suffering from nervous debility and is quite unfitted to undertake any public engagements outside his own pulpit work for the next three months. (Signed--J.J. Barrett, MD)" (1888, 299)

Five years before, when forced to be away from his pulpit the newspapers called it "rheumatic gout," but Spurgeon said that a substitute preacher friend was "nearer the cause of our infirmities than most people have been able to do" when he wrote in a letter: "Your congregation... is an overwhelming responsibility. I do not wonder that continuous labour in it tells on you and in ways you may not suspect. I do not envy the man who can preach there without having his whole nature strained to the utmost and that means nervous exhaustion, of all others the most difficult to contend against." (1883, 461)

Nervous exhaustion through pressure of work frequently became depression on account of prolonged physical pain, persistent criticism, and pressing duties to perform. Even before the "down-graders" set about him and passed their cruel vote of censure he often had to enter in his "Notes:" "I have been very ill for more than five weeks, and during that time I have been brought into deep waters of mental depression." (1881, 92)

Earlier that year he had reviewed a book called *Deep unto Deep: an Enquiry into some of the deeper Experiences of the Christian life.* Aimed at "tried believers who are passing through the deep waters of tribulation" he recommended it to young pastors since many of them knew insufficiently about "the pathology of the Christian souls... [and] the sore straits through which some saints are called to pass and the depths of anguish that others have to endure." (Ibid, 84) He gave as examples both physical infirmities and social bereavements which are common afflictions and "plunge the soul into deep grief." (Ibid.) We cannot help but feel he was writing his review from his own experience of "passing through the waters" in the same way.

## Spiritual anguish

Continuing his review of *Deep unto Deep* Spurgeon went on to list "the tortures that some experience, when old signs haunt their memory, even after they have had a sense of forgiveness" and also "the horrors that overtake others through the temptations of Satan." Such spiritual anguish was not to be "lightly thought of by those to whom Christ has committed the oversight of any church or congregation." The book listed such greats as Augustine, Bunyan, and Luther (and he might as well have included his own name) who "were tossed about on the stormy main: men of God, moreover, who knew how to tend sea-sick souls in every stage of their sad complaints... brought to their wits' end." (Ibid)

Spurgeon had a Puritan-style conversion, the act of "looking unto Jesus" preceded by several months of deep conviction of sin. This he continued to believe in as an integral part of conversion throughout his ministry. Reviewing the *Life and Ministry of John the Baptist* he was glad that the author had left nothing out "that is needful for spiritual nutriment." He was especially pleased at the emphasis on "the value of deep, humbling, self-abasing views of sin." How Spurgeon's emphasis is needed in our own days of easy-believism, I-feel-good-inside, I've-had-a-vision-of-light, and other so-called conversions. Spurgeon asked in his review, "How can he be healed who is not sick? The old-fashioned sense of sin is despised, and consequently a religion is run up before the foundations are dug out. Everything in this age is shallow... men leap into religion and then leap out again." (1882, 545)

Of course, with some temperaments this does lead to a morbid sense of introspection, but that was not so in Spurgeon's case. For him it resulted in a continuous sense of Satan's power and also of the Savior's greater power to give daily victory. It led him to mourn over any lack of conversions following the preaching of the gospel and also a feeling of spiritual depression when so-called

Christians became enemies of the fundamental truths of the gospel as during the days of the Down-Grade Controversy. All this became the way in to spiritual anguish from which there seemed to be no way-out for some weeks and even months.

Self-searching or soul-searching he advocated in a brief article in 1889:

> Those pains, those depressions, those losses and crosses. Were these black horses sent to bring with them, as in chariots of iron, "deep searchings of heart?" It is highly probable, and it would be our wisdom, and our relief, if we more voluntarily set about heart-searchings, and as the practical result, put away every evil thing. (1889, 23)

Writing a brief article to ministers on "Be not Discouraged," Spurgeon told them to beware of a low after being on a high, that is, after a successful time of soul-winning: "If not well watched, despondency will grow out of this, and the best workers for God will find themselves weak, weary and tempted to shun the service. This is to be dreaded and every means used to prevent it. Brethren, one who knows by experience what is meant by a downcast spirit, produced by ardent service, would warn you against bringing it upon yourselves." (1879, 571)

His own experience of being downcast was when insufficient funds were coming in for his institutions. He called his article in *The Sword and the Trowel* "Watching the Ebb." Drawing a parallel with Elijah at the brook Cherith and the incident of the floating axe-head, he asked: "Would the prophet of fire have known no damps of care? We cannot tell, but this we know, the devil has risen up from among the sand of the failing brook and hissed in our face such words as these--'The Lord has forsaken you.' Have we agreed with the foul fiend? The struggle has been severe in the soul, and the battle has pressed sore. We have no faith to boast of... we have none to spare and none to exhibit as a wonder... our faith is a poor starving thing which would utterly die if it were not kept alive by omnipotence." (1876, 542) And so his faith rallied, and he discovered "adversity acts as a tonic" and "watching the ebb, we have wondered what the Lord was preparing for us... God has great things in store if we can only believe." (Ibid)

Many a minister since has asked, like Spurgeon, "Why?" and although not discovering an answer, has yet found out that the Lord has greatly used his downcast spirit and spiritual anguish to help him assist others to come out of their depression and go on to serve the Lord faithfully and joyfully.

## Remedies and Treatment

It has been said that Spurgeon "believed in faith-healing but not in faith-healers." That is an incorrect judgment of the man. He certainly believed in *Jehovah-Rophi* ("I am the God who heals you") but at the same time, like his Savior when on earth, he believed in medical means of healing. Spurgeon relied on doctors when in physical pain and illness or in mental or nervous conditions.

Sometimes he was sent rather peculiar remedies by readers of his magazine. He once wrote: "We have in the course of many years received many most extraordinary prescriptions for our painful malady [gout]." One of the most extraordinary was when he was recommended "to keep a pair of turtle-doves or two young pigeons in our room." His well-wisher told him that "in the south of Germany they call turtle-doves 'gout pigeons.'" For himself: "we cannot see any connection between these loving creatures and the pains of rheumatism, unless it be that the noise of the birds would drive away the little remnant of sleep which remains to the sufferer, and so hasten the period which will end his anguish." (1885, 42)

We wonder what some of the other weird and wonderful remedies were, since he only hints at them when writing: "We have received many prescriptions for the gout, both for inward and outward application and should have been dead long ago if we had tried half of them." (1875, 92)

He was not averse to alternative or complementary medicine. He paid tribute to Mr. Sowter of the Hydropathic Institution, Beulah Spa, his next door neighbour: "We have had his careful attention in the use of Turkish, vapour and chemico-electric baths. Others who are similarly afflicted would find it to their advantage to come under Mr. Sowter's care." (1880, 623)

Of faith-healers he wrote: "In America, persons who make no profession of the Christian faith but are opposed to the gospel are working cures... Faith in charlatans seems to have much the same effect as the faith which is inspired by better men. This should, at least, cause our friends to look about them and make sure that they are not aiding and abetting a delusion." (1885, 508)

Regarding the popular proof text in the epistle of James about the "prayer of faith" he had to this to say:

> That the prayer of faith shall raise the sick we firmly believe, but that any man, or set of men, or any house has a special privilege in this line we gravely question. If friends who are subject to nervous diseases will believe that they are cured, there is no doubt that in many cases the disease will vanish; but that there is a miracle in that fact we refuse to believe. The fact is that we are in the period of *manias,* and unless we are very careful, we shall find ourselves in the snares of fanatical superstition. The unsettled condition of the church not only breeds infidelities but gross misbeliefs. Pretenders to prophecy, healing and other miraculous gifts are growing bold, and there is a more than usual readiness to tolerate their impositions. Happy are they who, with steadfast faith in their Lord, are not to be duped by the inventions of fevered brains." (1885, 508)

One comment on the above would be, "There is nothing new under the sun." Another would be, "Spurgeon was a man before his time." Certainly he could have written the above "Note" for any Christian magazine today--if the editor would dare to publish it.

Regarding orthodox medicine he was much more glowing in his "Notes" especially of doctors who had become personal friends. Just before setting out for Menton in January 1888 his "ever-generous friend" Sir William McArthur called to see him and stayed for tea and family prayer. He had "discovered some renowned gout-doctor and was anxious to deliver us into his care. He had come all the way from Holland House to see what he could do in the matter, and he was ready to bear any expense." It appears that Sir William died before Spurgeon's "Notes" came to be written and "kind soul that he was, we can hardly realize that we shall never see him again on earth! He was ever one of our most liberal helpers and a constant reader of the weekly sermons." (1888, 43)

In his penultimate year Spurgeon recorded a lengthy medical bulletin in his "Notes" in which he praised the conscientiousness of two medical practitioners:

> Dr. Kidd was called in to consult with Dr. Miller, of Upper Norwood... Dr. Miller has slept at Westwood every night, and Dr. Kidd has been in consultation with him every morning... All that medical skill, patient watching, and careful nursing could do, appeared, for a while, to be of no avail... On Friday, 17 July, a slight improvement was reported... and again on the following day, and also on the Sabbath." (1891, 465)

The dual ministrations of the doctors, plus the prayers "from all quarters" brought a brief remission, but almost exactly twelve months later the Prince of Preachers was called to Home to be with the Lord. He died at Menton, peacefully, in his hotel room. If it had been at Westwood would he have been admitted to a London hospital? He preached frequently in aid of the hospitals of the Metropolis, and he was made a governor of St. Thomas's Hospital, an Institution "which was so beneficial to the sick poor of the church." (1884, 377)

## Animal Rights

What was Spurgeon's attitude to the suffering and pain of animals? Would he have been a supporter of the Animal Rights Movement? Reviewing a children's book *Kindness to Animals* Spurgeon wrote:

> We wish well to all writers who try to teach children to be kind to dumb animals... (1869, 139) this little book may prevent the boys from growing up like their fathers... destroying birds and their nests, lashing horses, beating donkeys [and] torturing insects. (1877, 231)

About vivisection he had this to say in his review of *Physiological Fallacies*:

> Our heart bleeds, and our soul writhes in horror as we read descriptions of the unutterable cruelties practised upon animals not only by the old-fashioned demons of the olden times, but by educated mortals in black coats... We shall have a round of letters from doctors, but we cannot help it. If ever we go mad it will assuredly be through reading such papers as come from the pens of certain M.D.'s who dare to watch the agonies of rabbits, dogs and other animals. Can it be? Is it not all a dream? Did men who had mothers and wives perpetuate these accursed deeds?" (1882, 442)

## CHAPTER EIGHTEEN

# At Work and at Play

Spurgeon worked many hours a day and was proud to be acknowledged by the British workmen of his day as "one of us." Thus a large proportion of his congregation was made up of the working class, although he also appealed to business men, Members of Parliament, the aristocracy and royalty. Biographers seem agreed, however, that as a youth he was no athlete; he did not take an interest in school games let alone taking part and excelling at them.

### Solomon's simile

Spurgeon, when thinking and writing about the Christian at work, would certainly have agreed with the parallel King Solomon drew between the activities of the ant and those of the human race. Charles Haddon Spurgeon said so in a review of the book *Ants and their Ways*. First of all he "hailed such a book as this. Tales come upon us like dust-clouds in March, but such interesting facts as these refresh us like April showers." Already he knew a great deal about "ants and their antics" and said that "their example is so good in many respects that Solomon did well to say, 'Go to the ant, thou sluggard.'" While not admiring their "plundering, and slave-holding, wounding and killing" he must nevertheless have admired their industrious ways. (1883, 197)

### Spurgeon's colliers

If Spurgeon admired ants which spend a great deal of their time underground working, how greatly he must have admired coal miners for laboring in God's "cellars of the earth." When reviewing a book for young people entitled *Earth's Diamonds; or, Coal its Formation and Value*, Spurgeon acknowledged his great admiration for those whose daily occupation took them deep underground for "coal-extraction" where there were "explosions and breakings in of water." He described the life of the miner as "a hard and dangerous life... and happy it is for him when he knows how to enlighten the darkness of the pit with the lamp of salvation." Using mining terms in his review of the book he described the contents as "full of 'best nuts;' its contents 'well screened,' and consisted of 'best coals only.'" He urged young people to study the book; "it will make them thankful that they are not diggers of black diamonds." (1882, 439)

### Victorian chars

Today we would put the term in quotations ("char") and equate it with skivvy--both being rather derogatory terms for women engaging in menial, domestic tasks. More recently we have elevated the char to cleaning lady and given her more of a standing in life.

To Spurgeon no menial task was to be termed derogatory or degrading. He knew too much about the humble foot-washing and other menial tasks his Saviour performed for that. So when he wrote a short article on "Visiting the Poor" for his magazine, he singled out the Victorian chars and urged his readers to "pick up an acquaintance with a woman who goes out charing when she can get it." Such concern for the less-fortunate of society would inspire and excite "gratitude for our own favoured lot." "Down with barriers," he stoutly declared, "and let the rich and poor meet together, for the Lord is the Maker of them all." (1880, 18)

### The Lord's Day

Although Spurgeon believed in Sunday observance by workers, he did allow work on the Sabbath day for acts of necessity and mercy, as in Scripture.

On one occasion he took up the case of a man who was denied Communion because as a compositor he had set some type on a Sunday evening for Monday's newspaper. He devoted one-and-a-half pages in *The Sword and the Trowel* to the incident, comparing it to a man who "threw away [some] yeast for working on Sunday and killed his hens for laying eggs on the same holy day." Spurgeon "sat in the Assembly hall during the trial" and had a presentiment that the daily, secular newspapers would have a field day, "but we hardly thought that professedly religious papers would fall into the same glaring error." However, at the trial Spurgeon learned that the compositor had not just worked a few evening hours but had in fact worked since noonday, the usual worktime of newspapers compositors and so obtaining "by this Sunday labour a holiday on Saturdays, and thus [gave] up his Sabbath privileges in exchange for a Saturday holiday." Spurgeon concluded: "If this be tolerated in the Christian Church, the first day of the week would be no longer the day of hallowed rest and worship."

It was not as if other work, without having to work on a Sunday, was not open to this man. "He had voluntarily elected to work at the particular office which had chosen to make the Sunday its day of work and the Saturday its day of rest," and this evidence was not denied by the compositor himself. Spurgeon believed the man was dealt with leniently. Some people said that the man had been persecuted, but Charles Haddon Spurgeon replied that "of all cant, irreligious cant is the most canting," and as "an ordinary club has a right to expel a man who breaks its rules, surely a church is to be allowed to do the same."

Spurgeon commented that if the man had been a Baptist, he would have been dealt with at the next church meeting. Church discipline was more strict and severe in Victorian times. Today's Sabbath-breakers are not even given a place on the agenda, even under "Any other business." (1866, 321)

His Sabbatarian views are well expressed in a review of *The Pearl of Days*. "As a defence of the Sabbath, it will be extremely valuable," he wrote, commenting, "We wish we could see more care among Christians to give their servants the rest of the Lord's Day. Less cooking would be a great reform. Everything possible should be done to release every one from needless labour on the Lord's Day." But he did emphasize that life should be so ordered "to maintain... the spirit of the command, where the letter cannot be unreservedly carried out... The seventh part of time is due to divine worship and hallowed repose" (1889, 448).

"The Sabbath for Man" was the prize-winning essay among Wesleyans. Reviewing it Spurgeon said that "we do not remember anything better upon the Sabbath... amusement on the Sabbath for one class of society means slavery for the rest; and as Britons never will be slaves, let them not forego the day of rest." (1890, 533) How needful are his words for today when it is difficult to tell the difference between the world and the church on Sundays. Church picnics on the Lord's Day with rowdy games and a site chosen that is popular by worldly standards (the inevitable ice-cream van and swimming in a nearby lake or river) is becoming more and more common. Spurgeon would not recognize the churches of today as he watched them spending the Lord's Day "on pleasure bent."

## Holy days and Holidays

The Sabbath was a holy day for Spurgeon and should be kept according to the Scriptures. It was possible for the Christian who worked to observe a day of rest. But holidays for the Christian at play were another matter.

In an article "The Christian at the Seaside," Spurgeon stressed that time of holiday are also to be observed as holy days. "We have no more license to sin at Margate, or Brighton, or Scarborough or Dunoon than we have at home; and though the same eyes may not watch us, there is one all-observing eye for which we should feel the utmost regard." Holidays for Spurgeon should be times when the Christians can be "cheerful, genial unrestrained and at ease... the holiday is useless without it; but even when out of harness, a good servant of Jesus Christ will let his conversation be such as becometh the gospel of Christ." Liberty was license for the believer on holiday. In his article he gave guidelines for a Christian's behaviour on holiday: mini beach-missions, tract distributing and above all "not going to fashionable worldly churches... but seeking out faithful pastors of their own faith, and cheering them with their presence and with an extra contribution." (1867, 337, 338)

**Physical fitness**

At the end of his life, reviewing a book for young men entitled *A Good Start*, he says of the author:

> He makes more of athletics than is wise. If young men can enter into healthy sports--well and good; but there are quiet, thoughtful youths who have other leanings, and out of these have come some of the devoutest disciples and not a few of the ablest preachers. We say not a word against physical cultivation; but we fear that youths who are more studious than athletic, and too much occupied in necessary business to become apt at games, stand a chance of suffering a censure which they do not deserve if everybody talks after the fashion of some of these otherwise paragraphs. Manliness we do not deprecate, but godliness is better; and there may be more manliness in quitting the pursuits of youth, in some instances, than in becoming a leader of them... We are not the enemy of the gymnasium; but it is not part of the temple." (1891, 192)

> This is a lively, earnest little book, and its circulation will, we hope, do something toward stemming the tide of folly which is invading even the church of the living God. Tired Christians will find frivolous amusement a poor means of rest; we fear that many are more wearied by their play than by their work, and are more likely to be jaded by dissipation than by devotion. (1882, 35)

If only he could have envisaged the tired Christians in our morning services today. With a shorter five-day working week than any Victorian could have imagined possible, and yet believers getting to bed late Saturday night (or even early Sunday morning) on account of so-called Christian concerts and discos, the Christian at work and the Christian at play seem to be a reversal of roles since Charles Haddon Spurgeon penned his words in his magazines.

## CHAPTER NINETEEN

# Odds and Ends

There are a great many more autobiographical passages in *The Sword and the Trowel* annual volumes than are included in the previous chapters of this book. They are, in the main, too short to compile into separate chapters. However, they are important for revealing the attitudes, convictions and experiences of the unforgettable preacher of Victorian England. They are here listed in alphabetical order and not in order of importance. Some of them give us an insight into Spurgeon's thinking on matters relevant to his day and to ours, while others give the lie to misconceptions about him that have been perpetuated by various biographers who have not taken the trouble to research carefully these important magazines.

### Accidents

"Some Special Preservations Experienced" was the title of Spurgeon's article in his magazine. The first was in a hired carriage while traveling to and from a preaching engagement in Bromley, Kent. On the journey he had noticed that "a wheel rattled." On alighting he watched the coachman taking the carriage into the livery stables when "the springs snapped, and the forepart of the vehicle [parted] from the body of it." He asked himself, "Why had this not happened before?" A spectator commented, "It was not to be, and so it wasn't." For Spurgeon this was not the whole truth, rather "our impression was that a divine hand had been fulfilling the word, 'He shall give his angels charge over thee, to keep thee in all thy ways.'" (1886, 629)

Staying on the Isle of Wight with Mrs. Spurgeon in a rustic inn, complete with thatched roof, they left on the Saturday so that he might be in his pulpit on the Sunday. On Monday he read in the newspaper that on Sunday a tall elm had blown down in a storm and destroyed the very room in which they had been sleeping. "Had the holiday been a little extended, so as to include a Sabbath, I might never again have been permitted to speak in the name of the Lord," Spurgeon commented. There were no such words as "chance," "co-incidence" or "fate" in his Christian vocabulary, and he remarked to his readers: "A man is immortal 'till his work is done... when we have prayed to the Lord to preserve our going out and our coming in; He will surely keep us till the hour comes when we shall return to the Father's house." (Ibid)

On another occasion he was sailing in a friend's yacht at Rothesay. He was to preach there on Sunday and on Saturday was taken for a ride. Part of the harness broke, the carriage "ran upon the horse, and the horse ran away. It rushed down the hill like a thunder-bolt and became altogether unmanageable." Charles Haddon Spurgeon had "a distinct sense of the lamp-posts, which seem to stand in the road, flying by one after another." If the horse had turned left at the bottom, the carriage would have turned over, if it turned right, then a "rising mound" would stop it. It turned right and came to a standstill. "Was there no overruling hand in this? We all felt so at the time." (Ibid, 630)

On one of his annual visits to the south of France he traveled by a different train from his usual one; later in the day. Just before Boulogne an accident on the road halted the train. The earlier train, which he usually caught, was involved in the accident and many had been injured. "One bares his head in reverent gratitude and worships the Lord, in whose hand are all the ways of His servants." (Ibid)

**Agricultural Hall**

In 1867 the decision was made to close the Metropolitan Tabernacle for necessary repairs and decoration. For five Sunday mornings Spurgeon preached to 20,000 people in the Agricultural Hall, Islington. He described the experience in his magazine in a few telling sentences:

> We are now worshiping in the enormous area of the Agricultural Hall, Islington, which much reminds us of the great Amphitheatre at Milan. Paul was in such a place, we suppose, when he fought with beasts; it is our prayer that in these happier days those who have fallen almost as low as beasts, may yield to the gospel and be turned into men. (1867, 166)

## All things to all men

Charles Haddon Spurgeon was equally at home when speaking to the aristocracy or to women who went out charring. He preached in 1877 to more than a thousand stock exchange gentlemen, and this was followed by an address to 450 "hard-working men, coal-heavers and others." He commented to his magazine readers: "We felt equally at home with stock exchange gentlemen and coal-heavers and hope to find many more such opportunities of going outside all regular congregations." (1877, 90)

## America

Although too busy with his Tabernacle church and many institutions to accept an invitation to America, Spurgeon was very interested in the progress of Christianity in that country and very knowledgeable about American Christian authors; he reviewed many of their books in the magazine.

His first invitation was not from an American church or group of churches to come over to preach. It was from "an excellent American firm [which offered] the sum of £5,000 for twenty-five lectures, or at the rate of £200 per lecture. Further arrangements are also to be made for one hundred more lectures, as may be mutually agreed. We have declined these liberal proposals solely because our work is to preach the gospel and not to lecture. (1873, 236)

The churches in America loved him even though he felt he was unable to visit them. During a severe illness and period of recuperation in Menton in 1880 he wrote in his "Notes:"

> Just as we were retiring to rest one night, a soft pillow for our head and heart arrived by telegraph from the other side of the Atlantic. This was from New York Baptist Ministers' Conference. (1880, 89) This telegram was followed by a lengthy letter from the Conference Committee and was given in full in the magazine.

Another interesting letter from America was sent to him in 1882 by the "honoured widow of the murdered President of the United States." She had sat with her husband, General Garfield, in the Metropolitan Tabernacle, and reading his diary after his death she came upon an entry that said, "God bless Spurgeon! He is helping to work out the problem of religious and civil freedom for England in a way that he knows not of." (1882, 549)

His sermons were transmitted to America so that they could be printed in their newspapers on a Monday morning. He was not consulted on the subject, so he explained to his readers "we are not responsible for any extra Sunday labour that may be caused. We may add that we do not guarantee the accuracy of the reports of our discourses." They were, in fact, full of mistakes, and yet the readership was in excess of a million copies of newspapers. (1883, 394)

## Apocryphal anecdotes

Many are the apocryphal anecdotes about Spurgeon, some of them gaining veracity through much repeating. Some have been recorded and contradicted in previous chapters. In one magazine Spurgeon gave a paragraph explaining how such anecdotes originated. It was being said that Spurgeon was thrown off from a four-horse coach. "This is a dull generation which will not allow a metaphor, but must read all things literally. The prosaic and detailed narrative to which we allude all arose out of the preacher's saying concerning himself, 'My coach went over suddenly, and all the horses were down.' This was a simple simile, and it never entered his head that it could be taken literally. The season of the year was not suitable for coach-riding, and unhappily it is a pastime in which a London minister is at any season very rarely privileged to indulge. In this case we see the birth and growth of a story; in many other instances there remains a mystery. The world is so fond of fiction that anything will suffice as material to be hammered into a tale. Moral--Believe not one-half that you hear." (1891, 40)

## Aristocracy

Several of the aristocracy attended Spurgeon's Tabernacle and were on familiar terms with the great preacher. In one issue of his magazine, without any ulterior motive of name-dropping or currying favour, he referred to "several choice spirits [who] have been removed from the circle of our friends." They included "Lady Lush whom to know was to love... specially bitter is the grief of the poor to whom she was a generous friend." Next, there was "Sir Charles Reed, from whom we received a note which was not delivered till after his death... in it he [proposed] to call at Norwood, but ere he could pay the visit he was called home to our heavenly Father." Spurgeon noted that their "portraits appeared together in "Men of Mark" for that (June 1879) month." (1881, 241)

## Australia

Besides invitations to America, Christians in Australia, tried to wean him away from the Tabernacle. Spurgeon had a soft spot for those down-under for his own son Tom went there for his health's sake and also to minister as a preacher of the gospel. His reply was the same as given to the Americans:

> We beg publically to thank the churches for doing us this honour. Having well weighed the matter, we feel that we cannot at this time leave our post, if indeed we shall ever be able to do so. Our numerous institutions must be watched; the great congregation must be kept together, and the weekly sermon must continue to be published. These all require us to be at home, and our absences must be brief ones; otherwise we should enjoy beyond measure a trip to the Southern Sea. (1877, 490)

## Book at sea

An esteemed missionary friend, home on furlough, told Spurgeon how a number of shipwrecked sailors, having taken to their lifeboat, "were lost upon the sea for thirty days, with only nine days' provisions. Each day began with prayer and the reading of our *Morning by Morning*, which gave them great comfort. Divine providence caused them to be taken up by the vessel in which [the missionary] was sailing just as they were ready to perish." (1874, 341)

## Book reviews

Many of the autobiographical passages in our previous chapters have been taken from Spurgeon's book reviews in *The Sword and the Trowel*. He once explained his position regarding reviews in his magazine:

There are editors who butter and sugar their clients all round, and we recommend thin-skinned writers to send on their compositions to those amiable gentlemen; as for us, we do not belong to the Mutual Admiration Society and have a very unpleasant way of saying what we think, whether we offend or please. We have sold whole editions of a book by a favourable criticism, because the public believe that our reviews are honest and discriminating; such we mean that they shall be still, and therefore, take notice, ye who want nothing but approbation. (1875, 233)

In another issue he stated:

The publishers are ever ready to advertise with us, because they value our notices of their books. Necessarily short, our remarks are not, therefore, superficial: the utmost care is taken to judge correctly. We are not infallible, but we are indefatigable. Of course, our point of view is well known, and we do not pretend to look from any other; but a plain and honest statement of opinion is evidently valued, even though at times it may be unfavourable and therefore may be considered severe. We never yet heard of a drummer who could flog a man so that he liked it, and therefore we do not expect sharp criticism to be admired by the author who receives it; but, on the whole, we have been graciously tolerated even by those who have been disappointed. (1887, 641)

The year before Spurgeon died an evening paper criticized those who had charge of *The Sword and the Trowel* while he was away recuperating as being "more narrow than himself." What they did not know was that Spurgeon himself had written the review before he was taken ill. When he became too ill to write every review he suggested that the same critic might "amuse himself by trying to find out which reviews... were written by the editor." (1891, 540) And after his death when others were editing the present number, except the one relating to the *Life and Labours of Pastor Charles Haddon Spurgeon*, were written by the now glorified editor. He was so busy right up to the last, that we have several more pages of his notices already in type." (1892, 165)

## Book wanted!

Wanting to extend his vast library Spurgeon advertised for a missing volume in his magazine:

Wanted--*Dickinson's Theological Quarterly* for 1878. Our set of this work needs this volume to complete it. We cannot get it for money; perhaps love may discover it. Please do not send it on, but write a note if willing to supply the lack.--Charles Haddon Spurgeon (1884, 514)

## Bunyan

Walking through Bunhill Fields one day Spurgeon saw that the statue of John Bunyan erected over his grave was "rudely and savagely defaced... [his] nose is off, his face looks as if eaten into by disease." Yet it had been "beautifully restored in 1862," just six years previously. Charles Haddon Spurgeon did not think much of the practice of erecting monuments; they were "a waste of money." However, "if any one in all the earth deserved a monument, it was surely he who has left us one of the greatest monuments of sanctified and enriched genius--*The Pilgrim's Progress*." (1868, 376)

Spurgeon believed that Bunyan had suffered enough from "theological vandals, from those who have 'done' his famous book into wretched verse: from others who have produced a Catholic version of it, with a picture of the Virgin Mary in its title-page." (Ibid)

In the same way he disagreed with the Vicar of Elstow who wanted to erect a stained glass window as a memorial of John Bunyan. "Why not repair a Catholic chapel as a memorial of Martin Luther?" asked Spurgeon. He believed the vicar's plan was "out of all character. If John Bunyan's ghost walks the earth, it will haunt the church until the stained glass window is removed, if indeed it is every placed." (1874, 286) Placed it was, and we wonder how Spurgeon would feel about it today since the hostage Terry Waite received so much comfort from it in captivity when it was sent to him by a Baptist lady from Bedford. Reviewing a book, *Scenes beyond the Grave*, Spurgeon criticized the author for writing his book in the form of a dream, although it contained "considerable power of imagination."

His pungent comment was: "Dreams are not to our liking unless a man can see such visions as charmed the prisoner in Beford goal: he has monopolized the whole business of dreaming by having done it as no other man can." (1877, 42)

## Carey

William Carey, the "father of modern missions," was greatly revered by Spurgeon. When reviewing a new biography about him he wrote:

[He] has at last risen from the grave into which his son Eustace cast his memory. That many-adjectived worthy piled a vast heap of letters over his father's coffin, and called it a 'biography.' Never was so deadly a 'life' ever presented to the public. Dr. Smith writes in the happiest style... Carey rises before us in growing majesty. He believed in God like another Abraham, and thus he walked among his fellows a prince... each succeeding century will add new lustre to 'the consecrated cobbler.'" (1836, 139)

## Change of address

Like all prominent men Spurgeon came in for a great deal of criticism. They criticized his manner, his speech, his theology, his methods, and even the fact that he moved his house. When informing readers of his change of address, he remarked:

I would remark that I have removed under the advice of a physician, and at the earnest desire of many friends, solely on the grounds of health... Simple as the matter of change of residence may be, it has sufficed to create all sorts of stories, among them the statement that 'Mr. Spurgeon's people have given him a house.' My ever-generous friends would give me whatever was needful, but as I had only to sell one house and buy another, there was no necessity for them to do so. Having once accepted a noble presentation from them, and having there and then handed it over to the Almshouses, it would by no means be according to my mind to receive a second testimonial... It is entirely my own concern and a matter about which I should have said nothing if it had not been for this gossip. (1880, 487)

## Childhood

Biographers have always stressed that in early childhood Spurgeon seemed to exist on a diet of Puritanism found in his grandfather's library. When reviewing *The Child's Companion* he admitted: "This magazine was our companion when a child, and we always retain a warm side towards it. It holds a high place among the many penny juvenile magazine. The volume makes an attractive and cheap present." (1872, 89)

## Christians' "National Anthem"

Reporting on one of his evangelists and a successful evangelistic mission at Shoreditch, Spurgeon noted that "Mr. Smith sang Hallelujah for the cross! "We wish," he added, "all our friends would learn this noble soul-stirring hymn and make it the Christian's National Anthem. In these days of disloyalty to Christ, all who are true to Him ought to take special pains to show their attachment and devotion to His cause." (1885, 555)

It did, in fact, become the college anthem, the students of his Pastors' College singing it at public events. Sankey's *Sacred Songs and Solos* (1,200 pieces) contains the piece, being No. 1181.

## Creation

An ardent creationist and an enemy of evolution, Charles Haddon Spurgeon had little time for those who tried to find a middle ground. Reviewing a book entitled *The Twin Records of Creation, or Geology and Genesis,* he wrote:

> We have little sympathy with long and elaborate attempts to reconcile the discoveries of geology with the Mosaic narrative of the creation... The attempt to discover six periods of some millions of years in geological records, answering to the six days of the Mosaic creation, supposes an intention in Scripture to teach geology... We protest too against an allegorical interpretation of what is narrated as literally true as calculated to mystify our views and weaken our faith at the commencement of our Bibles in all that is to follow. (1876, 43)

He further developed his beliefs in the Mosaic account when

reviewing *The Ages before Moses*:

> Geology or no geology, the Mosaic narrative is to be taken, we conceive, in its own common-sense meaning. If there had been no geological science there would have been no attempt to explain away the six natural days of the present creation; nor is geology benefitted, while Scripture is grossly mutilated by it. No sooner are we out of this mist and away from the symbolical shadow that is cast over the simple narrative of the Bible, than we enter upon the clear perspective which it is our author's chief aim to place before us. (1880, 484)

### Crystal Palace Convert

The story of the man converted while working high up in the roof of the Crystal Palace is told by most biographers but not always in such a succinct way as Charles H. Spurgeon wrote it in his magazine:

> Our beloved brother [Dr. James A. Spurgeon] tells us he was greatly delighted on visiting a sick man lately to hear how he found the Saviour. He said that a few days before we preached at the Crystal Palace, in 1857, we went down to the building to arrange where the platform should be placed, and while trying various positions we cried aloud, "Behold the Lamb of God, which taketh away the sin of the world." This man was at the time at work in the Palace, and the text spoken under these unusual circumstances went with power to his heart, convinced him of sin, and led him to the sin-atoning Lamb. How well it is to utter great gospel texts, even when we are not preaching, for they are arrows from the quiver of God, and will not fly abroad in vain. (1881, 96)

### Debt

All his ministry Charles Haddon Spurgeon abhorred debt. He urged that the Tabernacle be opened free of debt, and it was. In the year before he died he was concerned that the Surrey Garden Memorial Mission Chapel be opened in the same way and stated in *The Sword and the Trowel*:

Up to the hour of going to press, we are still £272 short of the required amount. The day is appointed for the opening... but we have never opened any of our home buildings with a debt. Are we to do so now? No! please clear off this evil thing. Wipe off this stain. Never allow the word "debt" to mar a memorial of gratitude. Let the whole amount be at Westwood before the sun has risen on the 2nd of June (the day fixed for the opening). (1891, 348)

## Defending the Faith

Early biographers of Spurgeon, obviously with the Down-Grade Controversy in mind, often referred to him as "Mr. Valiant for Truth." In their eyes he was a Defender of the Faith. Spurgeon would not have agreed with them and would have eschewed the title.

That is obvious from a book review of *In Defense of the Faith*:

It is our impression that, where one person is led to saving faith in Christ by books in defence of the faith, a thousand are converted by statements of the faith itself. Truth least defended is best defended... Do not attempt to prove the existence of the sun. Pull up the blinds; throw back the shutters; let Him fill the room with His brightness. What demonstration can be more complete? (1887, 142)

## Discipline

In our back-to-basics era, with many trying to resurrect what they think was once typical British family life, with parents guiding, correcting, and disciplining their children, it is important to see that our situation today is not new. In a review of *The Well-being of Nations* Spurgeon said:

If family discipline were formerly too strictly enforced, it is too loosely regarded now. Social gatherings for amusement or instruction, and even for philanthropic and religious purposes, often entrench upon home duties, which must be acknowledged to have the first claim upon us. (1885, 374)

The author's intention was to show how "the well-being of nations... depends upon the well-being of individuals and families.

The best way to benefit the nation is to be diligent and conscientious in the discharge of private, relative, and social duties." (Ibid)

Spurgeon went on to show how this was Scriptural and apostolic and how these old standards needed to be revived in his day. And surely in ours as well.

### Depicting God

A favorite illustration with twentieth century preachers is of a little girl being asked by mother, "What are you drawing?" "God," came the reply. "But nobody knows what God looks like," replies mother. "They will when I've finished my picture," states the small girl--a story Spurgeon certainly would not have told. Pictures of God were anathema to him. Reviewing *The Catacombs of Rome* he warned his readers of a stained glass window of God the Father depicted as a Pope. Using strong words he wrote: "We are distinctly of opinion that the reproduction of it is wrong. We think we must blame the author first, and then the engraver, the printer and the publishers. No one has any right to make or copy any symbol of the invisible God. Paste a slip over it if you buy this book." (1888, 144)

### Doctorate

We should really head this paragraph "No doctorate," but during Spurgeon's lifetime, and subsequently, many have referred to Doctor Spurgeon. He was once sent an appreciative letter about his sermon No. 1,500 by a graduate of Madras University. He referred to Dr. Spurgeon who "excels all orators" several times. Reprinting the letter in his magazine Spurgeon commented: "O that God would by the sermon convert many of all nations, and he who is no doctor will be willing to be called either orator or a babbler if men are but saved." (1880, 426)

### Engravings

Most people who are interested in Charles Haddon Spurgeon know of his magnificent library, especially his collection of Puritan writers (now housed in the William Jewel College, USA). Few seem to know that he had a fine collection of pictures of the Reformation which he called his "Gallery of the Reformation." From time to time he held an exhibition of these, the admittance fees going to some such worthy cause as his Stockwell Orphanage. One such exhibition was held during the four hundredth anniversary of the birth of Martin Luther. Friends wanting to borrow the exhibition needed "nearly if not quite a week" to show them. "In the traveling-cases the pictures weigh nearly a ton and a quarter." (1883, 515)

Later that year there was another insert in the magazine (Mr. Spurgeon's Protestant Pictures) advertising this "collection of engravings, etc., illustrating the history of the Reformation." It had just been shown at the Orphanage and in South Street Chapel, Greenwich, Gipsy Road, Norwood and Southend. It was then moving on to the Pastors' College and the Exeter Hall (under the auspices of the Luther Commemoration Committee). It was then being sent up to the Midlands before being returned to London for the last few weeks of the year. (Ibid, 609)

## Fancy Dress

Another exhibition was held at the Tabernacle, this time the property of a missionary lady, was of dresses and costumes she had brought back from the Holy Land. It was described in the magazine as:

> A procession of ladies and gentlemen arrayed in bright Oriental costumes, and singing "Sound the loud timbrel." Mrs. Allison and her assistants took their places in the harem and on the threshing-floor which had been reproduced as nearly as possible and in the Bedouin's tent bought in Palestine. Pastor Charles Haddon Spurgeon assisted in explaining the passages of Scripture illustrated by the different articles, and a collection was made in aid of the Tabernacle Zenana Mission Auxiliary. (1886, 603)

## Family Worship

Like all evangelical Victorians Spurgeon believed in, and conducted, family worship. He wrote an aid for family worship which he called *The Interpreter*. Advocating its use in his magazine he wrote a brief article setting out the "benefits of family prayer when spiritually conducted... to parents, children and servants, it is a blessing." He pointed out that the Puritans would "sooner have gone without their meals than their family worship... If fathers are unconverted let mothers bravely take the lead, and let us hope that sons will grow up who will be glad to assist their mother in the holy exercise." (1872, 524)

### Fellowship with God

The believer's fellowship with God was even more important than family worship. A short article about it in the magazine was called "Water Lilies," and an engraving of a pond was above the piece. The lilies, for Spurgeon, were "fit emblems of those believers who dwell in God, who are not occasional seekers of divine fellowship." His own testimony was:

> The longer I live, the more sure do I become that our happiness in life, our comfort in trouble, and our strength for service--all depend upon our living near to God, nay, dwelling in God, as the lilies in the water... I would rather spend an hour in the presence of the Lord than a century in prosperity without Him. (1884, 487)

### Fletcher

Fletcher of Madeley was one whose secret of a saintly life was: "The man walked with God, and we are not concerned to know what kind of boots he wore." That was Spurgeon's estimate of the man after reading and reviewing *Fletcher of Madeley*--"not such a life of Fletcher as a Calvinist would write!" The final tail-piece of his review was: "Oh that we had more of that sweet, deep, heavenly holiness which made Madeley to be as the gate of heaven!" (1885, 551)

### French

Visiting France so frequently it was no wonder Charles Haddon Spurgeon was interested in the French language. Reviewing *French Made Easy* he called it French "made easy" and praised the author's phonetic method, saying that it was "impossible better to convey without speech the sounds of a foreign language," His commendation ended with these words: "If we kept school we should from henceforth never attempt to teach French apart from this book." (1880, 485)

## Fund-raising

Many evangelicals have criticized Spurgeon for his methods of fund-raising, especially his using of bazaars. In the very first volume issued of his magazine he defended his methods. He proposed to erect four places of worship in or near the Metropolis "in pity for the spiritual needs of the vast city of London." He wrote that he was going to "wait upon God by faith, at the same time to use all legitimate means. It seems to us that a bazaar, if properly conducted, is not an objectionable way of raising funds." Critics of Spurgeon today still have the same difficulty with his bazaars, and some who defend him use the "get-out" of saying that they were Mrs. Spurgeon's bazaars, and he merely supported her efforts. Spurgeon's defence was this:

> Our friend, Mr. Muller, of Bristol, has a sort of perpetual bazaar for the sale of articles sent to him for the Orphan House; and if care be taken, there is no reason why the making and sale of goods for the Lord's cause should not be rather a help than a hindrance to spirituality." "Goods," it should be noted, were not to be sent to Mrs. Spurgeon but "to Pastor Spurgeon." (1865, 121)

## German Baptists

The Metropolitan Tabernacle supported two missionaries in Germany. The Baptists there, according to a short article in his magazine, "have long been exposed to more reproach and persecution than any other body of Christians." Spurgeon's interest in them was "greatly stimulated by personal fellowship with some of their leading pastors, especially the well-known pastor of Hamburg."

That pastor's name was Oncken, perpetuated today by the German publishing house of J. G. Oncken Verlag Wuppertal and Kassel, publishers of the present writer's book, *Spurgeon on Revival* (Charles Haddon Spurgeon uber Erweckung), published originally by Zondervan's of Grand Rapids, Michigan, USA. (1865, 270)

## Greek

Spurgeon was a great advocate of Bible students being able to read the New Testament in Greek. Reviewing *Greek Vocabulary in the New Testament* he wrote: "Even where the Greek Testament has not been mastered in early life, it is seldom too late to begin." (1866, 381)

At another time and reviewing a different book, *The New Testament in the Original Greek* he commented:

> The more reading of the Scriptures the better; and it is best of all when that reading occupies itself with the original. Every member of our churches, who has a fair English education, should aim to acquire sufficient Greek to read the New Testament; we specially include in this exhortation our sisters in Christ. Every vestry should have it in their Greek class. (1885, 431)

And in reviewing *A Greek Testament Primer* he wrote:

> It is a great pity that more Christian people do not resolve to master New Testament Greek. It would be an infinitely more profitable use of time than that which is found in the fashionable recreations of the hour, or in reading the superabundant fiction of the period. (1888, 438)

### Greeting cards

Not only did Charles Haddon Spurgeon review books, but selections of Christmas cards and New Year cards put out by the Religious Tract Society. Of them he said, "We hope that the habit of sending out cards at the festive season will not die out." (1888, 608)

### Gipsies

On one occasion he took a trip "in a gipsy's van" with the author of *The Gipsy Queen*. Reviewing the book he stated:

> While in company with our author... we learned sufficient of their art to be able to tell you, "pretty lady," or you, "handsome young gentleman," this much of the future—that if you will cross the book-seller's hand with silver, you will get a pretty book, which will make you pity and pray for these poor wanderers and wish God speed to George Smith and others who try to find them and lead them to the Saviour. (1885, 501)

We wonder what his attitude would be today about the "travellers" and whether he would be engaged in some evangelistic effort at Glastonbury. Certainly he would not shun them as so many Christians appear to do.

## Holy kiss

Reviewing a book on *Kissing: Its Curious Mentions* Spurgeon asked his readers to believe that it was serious and not amusing. He quoted at some length what the author had to say about the New Testament holy kiss and said that he endorsed fully what was said, that is, "if the Holy Spirit had been writing in our age and clime... He would have commanded believers to 'salute one another with a holy shaking of hands.'" (1885, 376) A pity some of the charismatic leaders do not understand that today. There would be less embarrassment all round and less danger of emotional entanglements occurring.

## Insurance

Some Christians are not too keen on insurance, looking upon it as a form of gambling. They think that God can look after their lives and possessions and that it shows a lack of faith to insure themselves, their houses and contents and their personal possessions. Yet by law they are compelled to insure their cars.

For Spurgeon the issue was clear-cut:

Married people should make provision for their families by life insurance... it is a sin for those who have the means to pay for insurance to neglect making needful provision. Persons with a fair income ought not to spend all that they have and leave their children to be taken care of by other people. (1880, 205)

## Jews

From Spurgeon's *Notes* in *The Sword and the Trowel*:

Outrages on the Jews--All our sympathies are aroused for the Jews who are being brutally treated in Russia. One is made to blush for the name of Christian when we see it mixed up with murder, plunder and ravishment. The long catalogue of Russian atrocities is enough to move a heart of stone. That followers of the Lord Jesus should hound to the death the nation from which He sprang according to the flesh is a strange perversity of ignorant zeal which all true believers should deplore day and night. Let the house of Israel know assuredly that all real followers of Jesus of Nazareth desire the good of their nation and lament their persecutions. We pray that Israel may accept the Messiah whom we reverence, but we cannot hope that this will be the case while so much wrong-doing is perpetuated against them. (1882, 97)

## Legacies

Twentieth century tele-evangelists have had a bad press on account of some of them not giving an open and above-board statement of their finances. Spurgeon, too, was criticized about finances. Certain newspapers charged him with having spent legacies given for his institutions. He was not accused of stealing them for himself but of giving them away. He stoutly denied all charges:

We have never done so; and never shall. A man may give away what is left to himself personally; but to do the same with money of which he is only a trustee would be clear robbery... We have no power to do otherwise with money left to a charity than to use it for that charity: we cannot alienate a penny without acting fraudulently... Not a farthing will be used by us in any other way than the will of the testator prescribes. (1890, 393)

## Lending library

There is at the Metropolitan Tabernacle a Society for lending out the Pastor's Sermons to residents in the neighbourhood. It is not an expensive form of service, for the work is done by willing volunteers, and the outlay consists of the purchase and binding up the sermons. About £30 keeps the simple machinery going; though amid the multiform agencies which have their head-quarters at the Tabernacle this minor one gets rather pushed into a corner, and sometimes, in past years, has had to sue to the pastor for his personal assistance to keep it going. (1878, 85)

This was a Society that brought rich consolation... to his heart. Then followed a number of reports of blessing received by those living around the Tabernacle who borrowed the sermons and read them.

## Liturgy and gowns

Reviewing a book by Dr. Newman Hall he said of the author, having commended his book, "He is fonder of a liturgical service than we shall ever be; but we have no quarrel with him on that account for he loved the gospel, and therefore we can forget his gown and prayer-book... he remains true to the doctrine of the cross and declares the gospel more boldly than ever." (1888, 141)

## London

Though an Essex man and a lover of the countryside, Spurgeon ministered for over thirty years in the Metropolis. In the last twelve months of his life, when reviewing a book entitled *How London Lives*, he wrote:

London overwhems us. We cannot ride through its streets, mile after mile, without a sad heart. What a teeming mass of humanity! Everything about this greatest of cities is worth knowing. Here is a book, most plentifully and pleasantly illustrated, which tells us how London is fed, cleansed, lighted, kept in order, nursed and waited on. (1891, 194)

## Lotteries

A Baptist church in Wales actually proposes to hold a lottery for the payment of its debt and tries to sell its tickets by the plea that it is for the cause of God. These people, no doubt, think they are doing a good thing, and in all probability they have never realized the demoralizing influence of such forms of gambling. Happily the law of the land is more vigorous against these evils than it used to be, and raffles and lotteries lay the parties open to prosecution. We mention the subject, not to censure those who have ignorantly erred, but for the warning of others. (1885, 147)

What would he say today with most denominational churches raising money by such gambling methods as tombola, bingo, guess the weight of cakes, etc., and raffle tickets incorporated into the entrance money.

"It is astonishing how slowly the first principles of a moral education are learned by certain minds," commented Spurgeon. And how quickly ethical principles and morality among our churches has deteriorated within a hundred years.

### Marriage

A monthly magazine called *The Shaker* was sent to Spurgeon for review. It was a strange production with "denunciations of matrimony" abounding in its pages. Spurgeon's comment was:

"In these days of anti-this and anti-that, we do not marvel that there is even a sect which is anti-marriage." (1872, 89)

By contrast he received a letter from New Zealand begging his influence in finding him a wife, "preferably a widow." The man went on to write that they needed "ship-loads of widows out there." Spurgeon, however, did "not feel that [he] could enter the match-trade" although it did occur to him that with so many thousands of good women starving in Britain if only they emigrated to the colonies "their price would literally be 'above rubies.'" (1885, 147)

Reviewing *The Calling of a Christian Woman* he said that "we fully do agree with [the author's] horror of American divorce, but do not consider marriage to be a sacrament." (1884, 552)

### Matthew Henry

Spurgeon held in high regard Matthew Henry's Bible commentary, as do many evangelicals today. Very few seem to realize that Matthew Henry did not complete the commentary on the New Testament and in reviewing it Spurgeon remarked:

That which was done by others to complete the work is of inferior value. The publishers ought to appraise their readers of this in due time. (1886, 36)

## MTP translation

The Metropolitan Tabernacle Pulpit, Spurgeon's printed sermons, were translated into many foreign languages. One that was a particular delight to him, and for which he asked the prayers of his magazine readers, was a translation into "the Servian tongue, and sent to each of the twelve hundred priests and teachers in that country." There were no Protestant preachers in that country at that time able to speak the language, "and the Greek church [was] in an extraordinarily dead state." The translator, Mr. Mijatovich, was spoken of in the highest terms for his able translation.

## Ministry

Spurgeon had very decided views about the Christian ministry, both lay and ordained, as they are known by today--not that he liked either term. He himself was not ordained through the laying-on of any man's hand, believing in "the ordination of the pierced hand." It may seem surprising, but he gives us insights into his conception of the ministry when reviewing a book entitled *Commenting on the Holy Scriptures: Critical, Doctrinal, and Homiletical.*

It was a commentary on the Book of Romans, and he began his review by stating, "We have never seen a critical commentary more to our mind than this one." One point on which he disagreed with the author, J. P. Lange, DD, was with his statement that it was inconsistent to connect "any secular calling with the holy ministry."

Spurgeon's reply was:

We had always regarded the apostle [Paul] as being a tent-weaver, ministering with his own hands to his necessities and the necessities of those that were with him... away once and for ever from our midst with the notion that ministers should be a clique of non-workers, whose priestly dignity would suffer if they endured a day's toil. Thank God we have some men who to serve him work hard all the week and preach on the Lord's day, and they are as consistent ministers as those of us who can, by the liberality and gifts of our churches, give all our time to the direct ministry of the Word. The ordination of a DD we have no doubt needs the help of man, as we have not found it yet in the Bible; and we can conceive that anything so undignified as gathering up sticks for a fire, or casting out the lading of a ship, would be inconsistent with such eminence. (1870, 140)

## Ministers' manual

Another thing that was anathema to him connected with the ministry was the publishing of ministers' manual or a *Book of Offices*. When he reviewed such a book written for nonconformist ministers he offered an alternative title--*The Conformity of Nonconformists*. Forms of service for Baptism, the Lord's Supper, marriages and burials, with hymns already chosen, prayers already written, and addresses already composed, he could hardly believe what he was reviewing. The prayers were "chiefly taken from the Common Prayer Book," so Charles Haddon Spurgeon asked "why not complete the design with liturgies and prayers for the regular services of the sanctuary and notices where ready-made sermons may be obtained for a very reasonable consideration?" He suggested that "if there are ministers who are unable to conduct such services without a printed form, they should leave the work to those who can."

And a final comment would make many ministers today doubt their own spirituality:

These Sacramental Services, as they are called, will come into general use when ministers of Nonconformist Churches have no minds or souls of their own; but we hope not till then. (1885, 39)

## Miracles

"We are among the simple people who believe that when Joshua bade the sun stand still there was a real prolongation of the day, and we are somewhat startled to find the editor of this new periodical *The Expositor*, the first issue of which Charles Haddon Spurgeon was reviewing commencing his first number by putting this down as a 'childish blunder.' We do not believe him one bit. We like to hear him explain, but not to explain away." (1875, 89)

**Music Hall**

Spurgeon's services in the Surrey Gardens Music Hall were greatly blessed. Some years later he proposed building a mission station named "Surrey Gardens Memorial Hall." Urging gifts towards the building fund in his magazine he pointed out that "in the Music Hall so many found the Saviour... all classes heard the Word... from the Prime Minister downwards. At no time have so many of the aristocracy made acquaintance with Nonconformist worship. As for the multitude, they were always there in force; and these, not only from the religious section of society but largely from those who never went to public worship. The reading of newspapers before the commencement of service, though in itself objectionable enough, was the proof that those were present for whom the services were designed... Though the Hall is so swept away that not a wreck remains, it will never cease to hold a place in the memory of those to whom it was their spiritual birth-place, and they are very many." (1890, 554) An interesting brief history of the original Music Hall is then given and those with access to the volumes of *The Sword and the Trowel* will find it well worth while studying.

**Nature lover**

Reviewing *The Handy Natural History* Spurgeon wrote:

Our readers who are not naturalists will bear with us if we say that they neglect one of the most fertile fields of study. We have a thousand times found our surest recreation in going to the ant or the bee or in reading stories of lions or dogs. We prefer an hour of zoology to all the novels that were ever inflicted upon this much-enduring age. Fiction is the alcohol of the mind, but natural history yields draughts of pure water from fresh and sparkling fountains. (1886, 641)

Commenting on *Our Four-footed Friends* and *Stories and Pictures of Birds, Beasts, and Fishes* he said:

By such books children are taught kindness to all living things, and this lesson needs constant repetition. What cruel creatures boys are! We see them hunting cats in the street as if it were a sacred duty. As for a frog or a newt--what eagerness to crush it! There is an improvement, but there is yet sad need to rebuke the brutality of many men, and to prevent similar savagery being perpetrated by their sons. (Ibid)

We have already suggested under a previous heading that he would probably have supported the animal rights campaigners of our day.

## Newspapers

His assessment of the type of news pandering to popular taste could have been written for our own day and generation:

The appeal to the newspapers to abstain from inserting details of disgraceful immorality has our warmest sympathy. Still, we fear it will be of little use so long as there is a public to which filth is a delicacy. Nothing so much affects proprietors and editors as the rise or fall of the circulation of their papers. All decent people should resolve never again to purchase a journal which has polluted its pages... A public conscience still needs to be created; and yet our impression is, that a daily paper, which should exclude not only everything disgusting, but also everything inconsistent with pure morals and true religion, would find many more supporters than some suppose. (1887, 90)

## Open air preaching

Those who would know Spurgeon's how-to-do-it of open air preaching (or as he termed it, Street Preaching), should read his *Lectures to my Students*. However there is an illuminating brief article in his magazine on the subject. He began with these words:

I am persuaded that the more of open air preaching there is in London the better. If it should become a nuisance to some it will be a blessing to others, if properly conducted. If it be the gospel which is spoken, and if the spirit of the preacher be one of love and truth, the results cannot be doubted: the bread cast upon the waters must be found after many days. (1876, 551)

Then follows his treatment of style, and action, covering such matters as illustrations, short sentences, withstanding heckling, the avoidance of mannerisms, and a very practical matter--keep the eyes open, otherwise certain possessions might be stolen.

## Oxford University

Charles Haddon Spurgeon used to be fond of saying that "I was a Cambridge man but never a member of the University." Nonconformists were denied Cambridge University places in his days of teaching at school there and preaching in the Cambridgeshire villages. About Oxford he said:

> We are not very eager to see our Nonconformist youth at Oxford. It is an experiment which has seldom been successful; if by success be meant retaining Puritan piety, and adding thereto superior scholarship. Yet, we do not know that anywhere our young men could do much worse than at certain Dissenting Colleges which are simply Factories of Doubt. (1890, 39)

His strong words about Oxford University appeared in a review of the tenth edition of *The Students' Handbook to the University and Colleges of Oxford* which he called invaluable. What is striking is that he should have been sent the book to review by the publishers. They must have held his opinions in high regard, although a nonconformist, for them to have sent such a volume to him for review.

It also means that they knew how far-reaching an influence his magazine had, in fact he began his review by saying: "We are not ashamed to compare our constituency with that of any other magazine now published; for the quality of its readers could not be surpassed." (Ibid)

## Pacifism

"God speed the pens which write for peace, and dry up the quills which in glowing terms write up the pageantry of war." (review of *The German Drummer Boy; or The Horrors of War* 1871, 131)

"Our heart chides us if we have failed to urge upon our readers and hearers the absolute sin of every kind of war." (Ibid)

"The poem on war (The Mad War-Planet) pleads vehemently, eloquently for peace. Would to God its voice could be heard. It ought to call the Christian church to do her duty as to war, and that duty plainly is to denounce it utterly and without reserve." (Ibid)

"No one can have a conception of the horrors of a battle-field unless he has seen one; but this little book helps to its realisation and fills us with sickening loathing of all war. May many read, and learn to hate bloodshed, through these pages." (1882, 148 review of *Christianity and War*)

"We do not like the combination of soldier and Christian which leads to the shooting or hanging of men in cold blood... war is a horrible business, look at it how you may... may wars cease to the ends of the earth" (review of *Life of General Gordon* — Ibid, 508).

"Oliver Cromwell and Gordon are two of our heroes, but we trust that other Christians will only follow them so far as they followed Christ." (review of *Gordon Anecdotes* 1885, 374)

**Parliament**

"There is not, and never was, a shade of truth in the report that we contemplate attempting to enter Parliament... the man who obtained a penny a line for that paragraph needs never to be short of small change, his imagination must be most active." (1872, 336)

If he had entered Parliament he might have been able to alter the parlous state of it which he describes in a review of *Traveller's Talk on England's Crisis*:

The worst foes of liberty at this time are those members of the House of Commons whose tactics are making Parliament ridiculous and the working of the Constitution impossible. It is time that men of all parties should combine in the resolve that national business shall be conducted in a manner worthy of a great empire: At present we think certain of our senators might learn improvement in the way of manners even from a pot-house club. (1884, 288)

Perhaps it is as well that he did not live in the twentieth century to see the school-boyish behaviour of the House of Commons portrayed on television.

## Pilgrim's Progress

In his sermons Spurgeon frequently drew upon Bunyan's *Pilgrim's Progress* for the purpose of illustration. In his magazine, reviewing a new, cheap edition of Bunyan's immortal work, he wrote:

> We cannot have too many editions of this book. Most heartily do we wish it God speed. To commend it would be an impertinence. The printer and artist have done their best, and for half-a-crown our readers will have a beautiful volume of choicest reading. (1871, 285)

## Poetry

Spurgeon's aversion to bad Christian poetry are too many to list, as are his allusions to the poets themselves. Apart from a few choices sentences we shall merely list some interesting magazine references for the interested reader to look up for himself:

> 1866, 293--a poem by Charles Haddon Spurgeon himself; 1875, 317; 1882, 413--famous "waste-paper" passage; 1880, 134--The Poems of Frances Ridley Havergal reviewed; 1884, 32--another waste paper article; Ibid. 351--fireplace a suitable receptacle! 1886, 553--reference to poetic son, Thomas.

> "It there any rule for writing poetry"?--"Yes, don't! "So has a wise editor settled the matter." (1883, 390)

> "The Story of Jesus, in verse" (a review): "A jingle of words." (1867, 140)

> "The Beauty of the Great King"--poems reviewed. "Poems so different in subject and style... some we like rather for the author's sake than their own." (1870, 188)

> "Poetry again! This grunt rose as naturally to our lips as the words cold mutton again!" Then followed a lengthy review of *Religious Poems*, ending with: "After thus easing our mind we feel better, and in a gentler mood." He finished his review

by stating that some of the poetry was "endurable" and some can be read "even with a degree of pleasure... we have read many verses which are a great deal worse than these." (1874, 578)

## Politics

Although Spurgeon did not preach politics from the pulpit, he frequently commented on politics in his magazine. He admired Gladstone and commended him for "the grand blasts from [his] war-horn" seeking to arouse the British nations, calling them to "make righteousness and peace the guides of the nation instead of selfishness and blustering... Time was when high principle ruled British hearts, and all parties in the State paid homage to liberty, to justice and even to humanity; but now we are another people, ruled by other lords." (1880, 40, 41)

He did not "consider it to be [his] duty to discuss politics in *The Sword and the Trowel*, but he felt that "in answer to many friends [he felt] bound to express [his] great regret that the great Liberal leader should have introduced his Irish Bills." Charles Haddon Spurgeon just could not see "what our Ulster brethren have done that they should be cast off. They are in great dismay at the prospect of legislative separation from England; and we do not wonder. They have been ever our loyal friends and ought not to be sacrificed. Surely something can be done for Ireland less ruinous than that which is proposed." He went on in the same vein and wonder what he would have said in even greater regret if he could have foreseen the Irish situation of our own day and time. (1886, 294)

## Portrait

While recuperating at Menton in 1886 he was persuaded by his publishers, Messrs. Passmore and Alabaster, to have his portrait taken. He considered "the result [to be] the best likeness ever taken" and the "clear light [was] a great help to the photographer, hence his success." (1886, 194)

## Practical Christianity

Spurgeon was not one of those Christians who was so heavenly-minded that he was of no earthly use; his institutions and philanthropic societies are proof of his practical Christianity. Printing an article in his magazine called "Lost Children at the Crystal Palace by One who saw them Found," he added a footnote saying that the motive behind printing the article was this:

Many persons set small store by any service unless it has a spiritual aspect. It seems to us that our Lord gave more prominence to cups of cold water, and garments made for the poor, and caring for little ones, than most people do nowadays." And so he recommended that Christians "attend to those humble, unobtrusive ministries which are seldom chronicled." He gave example of such practical Christianity: "show strangers into seats, cut up bread-and-butter at tea-meetings, place forms in the aisles, or lead blind people to service... we want more Christian ministries of the practical sort." (1883, 425)

## Queen Victoria

Although Oliver Cromwell was one of Spurgeon's heroes, he was a royalist at heart. Reviewing *Victoria: Queen and Empress--A Jubilee Memoir* he said,

Thousands will be glad to know all about the Queen and her family life. Loyalty is by no means extinct, although we frequently regret to hear criticisms which cannot possibly answer any useful purpose. Neither by foolish adulation, nor by idle carping, is it wise to create or foment discontent with the powers that be. We have abundant reason to be thankful for the peace and order which we have enjoyed during the memorable reign of Queen Victoria. God grant that we may not have to learn the value of our blessings by the loss of them! (1887, 290)

A salutary lesson there for many of today's critics of the British royal family's head--a lesson that needs to be learned today by the media, the tabloid press and television in particular and profit-seeking publishers in general.

## Reading on the train

Spurgeon the preacher and writer was also Spurgeon the reader; from a very early age in his grandfather's manse the habit never left him. Being a man for "redeeming the time," he read at every opportunity, easily becoming absorbed in a good book. He began reading *Ecce Homo* by the Rt. Hon W. E. Gladstone, MP for review in *The Sword and the Trowel*. This was his reaction:

> We shall never forget the day in which we fell in with *Ecce Homo*. We were starting for York, and we opened the book as we left the London terminus. How the train proceeded and at what stations it stopped, we never knew: having taken one plunge into the deeps of the book, we only rose out of them to consciousness when the northern city was reached. The memory is sweet to us. (1886, 545)

## Religious papers

He did not find religious papers quite so absorbing as Gladstone's book. Staying at Menton he wrote for his monthly "Notes" in the magazine:

> We are thankful that no religious papers reach us here, for they are usually the least satisfactory of publications, and certain of them are among the heaviest afflictions of the church of God.

There were two exceptions: "Happily we do not here refer to either of the two Baptist papers." (1878, 141)

## Reverend

"What a noise bishops and ministers are making about the silly title of Reverend. If we had not long ago abjured it, we certainly would now. It seems to be a trade mark of priests." (1884, 439)

But he did not "abjure" it on college, orphanage and colportage annual reports. Even in the year of his demise (1892) it was on the

Colportage Report as The Late Rev. C. H. Spurgeon. Surely he could have put a stop to his own institutions using it.

He referred to his aged father as "Rev," excusing it thus:

> We object to the "Reverend" for personal use, but we give it to the patriarchs as their right (thou shalt reverence the hoary head), and to our father as being heartily revered by his descendants." (1884, 471)

He did say that "it was a help to the postman" but he preferred the term "Pastor." His college he called the Pastors' College, but the college was not named after himself as a pastor. It was a plural pastors' college, for the training of pastors, not reverend gentleman, and most of his students when entering on their first pastoral charge used the prefix "Pastor". It is only since the days of ecumenism that "Rev" has become so popular, each denominational minister wanting to be as "reverend" as their Anglican counterparts.

## Review of reviews

Surely the best of his trenchant reviews must be this:

> Many of our modern theological treatises are so devoid of real substance that we are reminded of the chicken-broth which the sick husband returned to his wife, with the urgent request that she would coax the chicken to wade through it once more. (1866, 187)

## Secret of success

Many people stoutly believe that Spurgeon said that the secret of success in the ministry is to preach the gospel faithfully. Young men have become quite discouraged when they have been urged to do this at the start of their ministry, and their churches have remained half empty. Others have said that Spurgeon by "gospel" meant the five points of Calvinism. But there are Reformed Churches as empty and as lifeless as Armenian churches. So what did Spurgeon really advise?

Writing in his magazine "Notes" to An unsuccessful preacher he said:

> We do not hold that the preaching of the gospel will always

fill a place of worship. That belief would involve an unjust condemnation of many faithful men. But we do say that, other things being equal, no theme is so permanently attractive as the grand old gospel, and if a man cannot fill his place by preaching it, why then it does not go to be filled; or if it can be filled by other talk, no good will come of such a filling. When the gospel is droned out, or stuttered out, or spoken merely in dry, dogmatical form, without illustration, or freshness of thought, or warmth of feeling, no wonder that few desire to hear it.

Can some who set up for preachers reasonably expect many to hear them? If they could be impartial in reference to their own oratory, we would venture to ask them--Would you think it worth while to walk a mile to hear yourselves? Some men have such potent gifts of dispersion that even the attraction of the gospel is overcome by them: one feels that he could not even hear the most charming doctrine delivered in such a repulsive way. (1888, 43)

### Shaftesbury

On the death of Lord Shaftesbury he wrote in his "Notes:"

We have our own personal loss to deplore. We never had a truer friend, nor one with whom we have had more heart-to-heart fellowship. He had great fears for the future. His forecasts of the result of loose theology of the times were of the darkest order, and he had a similar foreboding as to the democracy which is gaining so much power.

It has frequently been our lot to cheer him, though we must confess we sympathized to a considerable degree in the fears which we sought to allay. Yet his faith in God, and in the unchanging Word, was as firm as a rock. Take him for all in all, we shall not look upon his like again. (1885, 601)

### Slavery

Spurgeon's sermons were burnt and banned in America becau
Spurgeon was so outspoken against slavery. He was just as pointe

his magazine:

> If to the long and disastrous struggle on the other side of the Atlantic we are expected to give a passing notice, we have no hesitation in recording our conviction that it is a just judgment from heaven upon a people who continued in the sin of slave-holding, in spite of the national freedom and religious privileges of which they have long boasted and the reproving and condemnatory glances of nearly all other nations of the earth... As both parties are implicated in the crime, and that which is least so, prevails but yet suffers grievous hurt; we think of the conflict of the men of Israel with the children of Benjamin, who in punishing others, were justly punished themselves, because of participation in their guilt... May the oppressed go free! May slavery cease for ever, and even this dreadful war will not be too dear a price for so great a mercy. (1865, 179)

**ns**

Susannah and Charles Haddon Spurgeon had twin sons, Tom d Charles. They both entered the Baptist ministry, and both came contributors to *The Sword and the Trowel*. Charles Haddon urgeon often spoke and wrote of them with great affection. One the unique ways in which he made mention of them was when viewing a book *Boys will be Boys*:

> By the way, it is not true that *Boys will be Boys*: we assert that they will not be boys long, and we can prove it by personal experience. Our own house is silent now. Where once two boys were heard laughing and sporting, all is hushed. One young man is in Australia, and the other is busy in his Lord's service at Greenwich; but they are boys no longer. Are we getting old? As we look on their mother we think not; but certainly we had two boys once, and we have none now, and therefore we assert that 'boys will not be boys' for ever, but will grow into men. God grant they may be happier as men than they were as boys. Why not? We have been so, and we believe many others are the same. (1880, 136)

## Spurgeon ships

On Wednesday, September 9, 1885, a fishing-smack was launche
at Brixham, Devon, named the *Susie Spurgeon*. A year previously on
had been launched bearing the name *Charles H. Spurgeon*. "Both M
and Mrs. Spurgeon have, from the first, evinced a deep interest
the well-being of the crews of these vessels, and sent them books f
the cabins. Mrs. Spurgeon has now worked upon the smack's burge
in white and yellow silk, the following lines:

This flag shall bear
Aloft my prayer
That good success attend you;
God save each one
By Christ his Son,
And from all ill defend you.

The *Susie Spurgeon*, when ready for her work, will be one of t
finest smacks sailing from the port. She is 93 tons register, built und
and classed A1 at Lloyd's for twelve years. God speed the good shi
(1885, 553)

Four years later it was reported that the *Charles H. Spurgeon* "h
endured exceedingly rough weather." A photograph w
reproduced in the magazine showing that "the damage is evide
to every eye." In fact, "it seemed done for, and indeed, had it n
been exceedingly well-built, it must have gone to the bottom." N
time was lost, however, in beginning repair work, and it was soc
restored "to its former glory." (1889, 275)

## Spurgeon's dog

One newspaper, a religious one, made up a silly story about
dog belonging to Spurgeon performing on stage. In his "Note
Spurgeon denied the story: "There is not a jot of truth in the matt
Mr. Spurgeon never possessed a Mont. St. Bernard dog; he nev
committed any dog of any sort to the care of a nephew, and he h
no nephew who has any acquaintance with gentlemen of t
theatrical profession. We can understand the motive for inventing
tale to advertise a play, but why a Baptist paper should give it curren

we cannot tell." (1887, 41)

### Stained glass windows

Reviewing *Images in the Windows of Churches: protest against them*, Spurgeon sided with the author in maintaining that "idolatrous tendencies are fostered by images in church windows." He felt so strongly about it that he said he should "like the opportunity of smashing the whole lot, old and new, whether in cathedrals or dissenting chapels." No wonder Cromwell was one of his heroes.

Even windows without figures in them, but merely pretty patterns of colour, he thought "too fine and showy and artificial for our ideal of a meeting place for spiritual communion with God... we have seen one with a crimson nose, another with a green eye, a third with delightfully red teeth, and a fourth with blue cheeks... we wish all Nonconformists would abstain from the superfluous decking of churches." (1868, 284)

### Stamped addressed envelopes

With the multitudinous correspondence he had to deal with every day it is no wonder he made the following request in his magazine:

We wish all our correspondents would remember that, when they write to us on business which is not at all our concern, they ought to enclose a stamp, if they expect a reply. The labour of answering letters that never ought to be written becomes an ever-increasing burden, and that being the case, we ought not to be taxed in pocket, as well as in time and patience, while we are prevented from doing what we might in the more important parts of the Lord's work. (1885, 645)

### Tea and coffee

When reviewing a rather strange book for young people at home and in school, *The Practical Moral Lesson Book*, he came across "warnings against tea and coffee, which might have been left alone." Regarding the section on tea he said that it was "more calculated to alarm rabbits and cats than to influence anybody else," for the author, an American doctor had been conducting experiments on rabbits and cats with tea, and they had died. Spurgeon concluded his review thus: "There, reader, tea-drinking reader, tremble for yourself and your rabbits and your tabbies! There is death in the teapot... Our earnest advice to the editor is to let our tea-tables alone, or if he must assail them, to do so without the help of this American doctor and his 10,860 cats." (1871, 236)

## Temperance

When Charles Haddon Spurgeon came to London he was a moderate or temperate drinker of alcohol. However, he soon became an abstainer and saw that his twin sons joined the Tabernacle's temperance league. The Tabernacle's communion wine was also non-alcoholic at his insistence.

He was always advocating teetotalism in *The Sword and the Trowel*, mainly through his book reviews. *Homes Made and Marred* was "a book to give a newly-married couple, and if it should lead them both to be teetotallers so much the better." (1873, 525)

When reviewing *Women and Temperance*, an American publication, he was not sure his American friends adopted the wisest course when they went to the saloons and sang and prayed until in whole districts every liquor-shop was closed; but we would gladly welcome any agency which would bring about such results in this country." He was more hopeful of the Band of Hope in Britain "training children" and reclaiming and educating adults "by means of the Gospel Temperance Movement." He hoped that through their methods "the British public [was] gradually being prepared for the total overthrow of the traffic in strong drink, for which we wait, and work, and pray." (1884, 192)

He reviewed his own denominational temperance organ and remarked that it gave him much pleasure to see the Baptists' "temperance work carried on so vigorously." He hoped that "all ministers of Christ will fight the demon of our country with all their might." (1885, 141)

His appeal was not so much to Scripture proof texts but to the Scriptural principle of self-denial. When reviewing *Temperance as taught in the Revised Bible* he said that "we think this an abundantly sufficient ground to go upon. [The author's] attempt to find total abstinence in Scripture is successful in some degree, but we cannot see teetotalism in many places where he sees it." (1888, 376)

Yet when reviewing *The Truth about Intoxicating Drinks* he said: "That good men can enjoy brandied concoctions and ardent spirits, and smile as if the Scriptures sanctioned them in their evil habit, is not to be explained except upon the charitable assumption that they know not what they do." (1890, 86)

Besides book reviews he also emphasized teetotalism by giving regular reports of temperance meetings at the Tabernacle. At one annual meeting of the Baptist Total Abstinence Association he was glad "to see that a majority of our own students, and indeed of all the men in our different denominational colleges, except those of Wales, are total abstainers." (1878, 315, 316)

He was absent from the first meeting of the Tabernacle Total Abstainers Society, but he said in his "Notes" that he believed that "next to the preaching of the gospel, the most necessary thing to be done in England is to induce our people to become total abstainers... I don't want you to wear a lot of peacocks' feathers and putty medals, nor to be always trying to convert the moderate drinkers but to go in for winning the real drunkards and bringing the poor enslaved creatures to the feet of Jesus, who can give them liberty." (1882, 201)

In the same volume, a few months later, writing about the same newly-formed Tabernacle society he said:

> The only hope of permanently reclaiming drunkards, and saving the church and the nation from the evils of intemperance, lies in the Gospel of our Lord Jesus Christ. This fact is fully recognized by the leaders of this movement... When we hear of tens of thousands in one town signing the pledge and taking the blue ribbon and learn that scores of public-houses and even breweries have been closed for want of customers, we thank God that at last the victory is being won, and we pray that the complete overthrow of the evil traffic may be speedily accomplished. (Ibid, 250)

In 1883 religious bodies put out a petition for the closing of public houses on the Lord's day. In his "Notes" Spurgeon "gladly expressed our hearty sympathy and prayer" with the effort. He added: "It may be questioned whether the people of London are ripe for it; but, at any rate, a trial could do no harm to anybody, not even the drink-sellers. Where Sunday-closing has been tried the best results have followed to the morals of the people and the quietude of the neighbourhood. Perhaps if our fellow-citizens were driven to the horrible necessity of going without alcoholic liquors for one day in the week they might lose some of their present dread of total abstinence and try it for the other six days."

That would not work in our day, of course, because the supermarkets with their Sunday opening would supply the lack. In Spurgeon's day there were no supermarkets and few shops opening on Sundays.

His final comment in the same "Notes" was:

> We do not care much for sobriety by Act of Parliament, but we do care for anything which promotes order, lessens drunkenness, and helps to tranquilize neighbourhoods where Sunday night becomes the terror of all quiet families. (1883, 202)

### Unhappiness

In a brief article in *The Sword and the Trowel* on the desire to move from a "post of duty" through feelings of strangeness, "irksomeness of a fresh position," and general unhappiness, Spurgeon gave this brief autobiographical note:

> We remember our first wretched night at a school where we afterwards became supremely happy. Well do we recollect the misery of the first few months of a calling which we afterwards valued and enjoyed. Our mind was sorely depressed on first coming into that sphere in London which has since been the delight of our life.
>
> Let no man, therefore, when he at first commences work in any place feel at all discouraged by the uneasiness which may come over him... Satan raises these discouragements to tempt [him] to leave a position in which [he] may damage his kingdom and glorify Christ... to turn tail under present pressure may be the beginning of a cowardly career, neither honourable to God nor to man: to stand fast at this distressing juncture may be the commencement of an established position of supreme usefulness and honour. (1880, 325, 327)

## Universalism

As universalism is appearing in England, and is even to be found in Baptist pulpits, it is well to have a good look at the intruder... a blight and a blast to all vital godliness... it is true that sinners are threatened with some temporary punishment, but they are told that in the end they will be restored. No doctrine can be more immoral or unscriptural. (1885, 10)

## Visual aid

Using visual aid when presenting the gospel is not an invention of twentieth century evangelists and preachers. It was used the Old Testament prophets and by Jesus Himself. Naturally in a building as large as the Tabernacle, and before the advent of helps such as overhead projectors, Spurgeon was unable to use it with his vast congregations. He was in favour of it, however, and used it in such lectures as "Sermons in candles." When reviewing books about visual aid for Sunday school teachers he always commended them:

Teachers may make good use of this treatise (*Through the Eye to the Heart*). Some will repeat the actual examples and be wise to do so; others will make lessons of their own and be wiser still. It should be immediately placed in the Sunday school library." (1880, 350)

About *"Children's Meetings, and how to conduct them"* he wrote:

We do not remember meeting with any better book than this for help in children's meetings. It is first-rate. There are objects to be drawn on the blackboard, but there are also capital lessons to go with them. Black boards get very black, and the children are very bored, when it is all chalk and no sound sense... The teaching of our youth should be as thorough and as attractive as it can be. (1886, 434)

## Witnessing

"When your merchant sends home your coals in sacks; an economical Paterfamilias likes to count the sacks; a grimy fellow comes to bring in the coals; cannot you have a word with that man about Jesus as well as about coals? Perhaps you have a printed sermon, or a tract, lying by on the shelf which the man might like to read... Mind you give him the expected coppers as well as the good Word, for a little liberality will help his memory wonderfully.

At another time you may run under an archway in a shower, and the crossing sweeper is there too; it will not waste your time to tell him of Jesus till the rain is over. Even a breakdown in a cab, or a railway accident, may bring you into contact with somebody you never saw or dreamed of before, and so afford you an unusual opportunity which may never occur again to you or the person thrown in your way... Resolve, "God helping me as I go to work, I will speak out for Jesus..." Perhaps you will scarcely know how to begin, but do not be very alarmed about that... almost any preface will do, for instance, "Have you seen that new book? And so poor old Smith is dead." (1866, 51ff)

### Women

Spurgeon did not believe in women ministers, but he did believe in women's ministry. He had some very useful and faithful and loyal women workers at the Tabernacle, not least Mrs. Bartlett, whom he regarded as "his right-hand supporter in Christian labour and never thought of her without the deepest gratitude to God for raising him up so zealous a co-worker." Her chief sphere of service was a young women's Bible class some 700 strong in attendance. (1865, 466f)

Reviewing *Agnes Graham, Deaconess* he said it was a "capital illustration of the text, "I commend unto you Phoebe, our sister, which is a servant of the church." He added, "We wish we had [a sisterhood of Agnes Grahams] in our own church, officially recognized, and we are glad that we have something like them without the name." He believed that women, if called of God, to perform scripturally acceptable service, then they should give up all their time to it. He gave as examples: "visitors of the sick, the fallen, the depraved, the dying... would not ministers do well to speak upon the subject and suggest the consecration of educated and refined women to such a holy and needful work? This wing of the army of faith might achieve great victories in the unselfish battle to bless the sinful sons of men." (1879, 188)

It seems only right that in these days when the church is in danger of being fragmented over the question of women ministers that Spurgeon's autobiographical notes in his magazine should end with his pointing out the many opportunities of Christian service open to women in the churches.